I'm in Junior High, but It's Not My Fault

By Senior Highers for Junior Highers

John Elmshauser, Editor
Illustrated by Ed Koehler

CPH™
SAINT LOUIS

Copyright © 1992 Concordia Publishing House
3558 S. Jefferson Avenue, St. Louis, MO 63118-3968
Manufactured in the United States of America

Library of Congress Cataloging-in-Publication Data
I'm in junior high, but it's not my fault/John Elmshauser, editor.
    Summary: Writing from a Christian perspective, teenagers explain how to survive the junior high years. Discussing such topics as study skills, sexuality, substance abuse, friendship, and witnessing.
    ISBN 0-570-04723-4
    1. Teenagers—Conduct of life. 2. Teenagers—Religious life. [1. Adolescence. 2. Conduct of life. 3. Christian life. 4. Children's writings.]   I. Elmshauser, John, 1950–   . BJ1661.I49   1992
248.8'3—dc20

                                                      92-7251
                                                         CIP
                                                         AC

    2 3 4 5 6 7 8 9 10 11   03 02 01 00 99 98 97 96 95

Contents

Acknowledgements

What a pleasure it has been to edit the work of so many young authors. I thank them on behalf of all of you who will profit from their work. There are some very important adults, who also made significant contributions. To Lou Jander and Les Schmidt, thank you for guiding us in choosing important topics facing junior highers. To the adults who gave guidance to the young writers, I give great hurrahs. Thank you, Al Gunderman, Randall Smith, Mary Beth Truebenbach, Elaine Whiteneck, Ben Freudenburg, Paul Otte, Marj and Art Maynard, Suzanne Collins, Brenda Zesch, Ron Brandhorst, Craig Parrott, and Ruth Geisler. The work you do for and with young people and their parents is a tremendous blessing to all of us!

Acknowledgements

As You Face Junior High . . .

There are certain times in our lives that seem to be so much more challenging than others. Sometimes, it just *seems* like they are tougher, but sometimes they really are difficult. The junior high, or middle school years, are one of those difficult times.

This book was written by some people who have only recently lived through their junior high years. They are in senior high now and remember clearly what those years felt like and how important it was to have friends in trying times. They have decided to become your friend, and share some of themselves with you in the chapters they have written about their middle school years.

I am certain that you will see in their writing some of their pain and hurt and joy and some of their growing too. It will comfort you to learn that we all live through times like these, and you will experience some great feelings too.

Reading this book will also help your parents. It is important for parents to consider the special trials of these years and work with you to develop some real solutions for getting through them with positive results.

Above all, the writers of this book point you to their greatest support. The love of God, the forgiveness and example of His Son, the Spirit's work in us every day of our lives means that all of our days have infinite potential. As you remember the victory that Jesus won for you on the cross, remember that He will help you face every challenge and make your junior high years truly victorious!

JOHN ELMSHAUSER

Do I Really Make a Difference?

by Marla Marlatt and Jennifer Watson

"You know, you don't even count. If you disappeared from the face of the earth, it wouldn't make a difference. You may as well not even exist at this school" (Emilio Estevez in *The Breakfast Club*).

If someone came up to you and said "You may as well not even exist," what would you do? Your first reaction would probably be amazement, because really, why would anyone want to say anything so incredibly rude to you? Then, you would most likely go through denial, because who wants to think *that* about themselves? But maybe, after a while, you would really start to think about it. Do I make a difference? Would anyone notice if I were suddenly gone? Would anyone care?

A couple of weeks ago our friend Sara and her family had a "family meeting." Her parents asked her what she thought about moving to Kansas. She hated the idea and told them so. They told her that they were moving anyway, because her dad got a job offer. She pleaded with them, but they would not change their minds. She did not like the idea of moving to a new town, a new house, a new school, and having to make new friends. Later that evening, she wondered why her parents asked her if she wanted to move, if her input made no difference in their decision. If no one listens, how does Sara know if she makes a difference or not?

Then there is Kevin. He is a nice guy if you get to know him well, but he is a real loner and does not have many friends. He does drugs occasionally and drinks heavily almost every weekend. He has tried to run away from home twice in the past six months. The thing is, he comes from a warm, loving family. Kevin does not think he makes much of a difference to his family.

But no matter how we feel, each and every one of us is here to make a difference in our own way. Who knows, maybe you will turn out to be the next Albert Einstein. You might discover a cure for cancer or AIDS. Maybe you have a knack for talking to people and helping them sort out problems.

There are many things you can do right now to make a difference. Take responsibility for your actions and make things happen! Make a difference in an older person's life by volunteering at a nursing home. Older adults love to feel appreciated by young people. Or you could volunteer to work at a hospital. You could go on walk-a-thons for charitable organizations, work at shelter houses, or start food drives. The environment could also use your help! Change your hairspray to non-aerosol. Recycle cans, paper, and glass, and you are making a difference!

The main thing to remember is that God has brought us all into the world for a purpose. Everyone makes some kind of a difference to their environment, friends, family, and to the people around them at school and church! It is incorrect to think you do not make a difference, because you do! God will help you make a difference in someone else's life!

Dear Lord, please help me to remember that I am Your special child, and I will always make a difference to You. Amen.

"I didn't hear anything. Did you hear anything?"

Feeling Stupid

by Anne Hall

For me, my first year of junior high school seemed to be one episode of feeling stupid after another. I had attended an alternative elementary school, and most of my friends from elementary school went to another junior high school on the other side of town. So, in my first year, not only did I not know anyone, but I was not used to a traditional school setting where everyone sat in desks, called their teacher by "Mr." or "Mrs.," and received report cards. I remember my first few months. Everything was so foreign to me, and I always felt a little lost and out of it. The other students seemed to be so with it, and always appeared to know exactly what they were doing.

I often felt that I was stupid because I lacked any sort of organization, and I invariably forgot about my homework. At the end of each school day, when it was time to get on the bus, I was in such a rush that I consistently forgot something I needed to do for classes the next day. And, speaking of the bus, I often missed mine. Then I would have to walk home, because the bus driver only gave us about two minutes to go to our lockers, talk to our friends, and catch the bus.

Other times when I felt really stupid were in those boy-girl relationships. It was so important to try and make a good impression for that "special person." I always felt like I would say the wrong thing or act stupidly when someone I was trying to impress was around. I felt even more dense because it seemed as if I were the only person who was really inexperienced about things like having a boyfriend or a girlfriend.

Clothes were another big problem. I felt silly wearing my plain clothes, which looked immature compared to what everyone else was wearing. I was an awkward size and did not fit into the clothes at the trendy stores. I hated trying to find anything in the children's departments. To me, everyone else seemed to look great, and I did not know which clothing to buy, or which styles were in fashion.

Sometimes I also felt slow in class. In some of my courses, it seemed that I was the only one who did not get what was going on. It bothered me that all of the other students seemed to know so much more than I did and acted so smart.

But, eventually I realized that I was not the only one who felt stupid or out of it. I often felt that everyone else was better than I, but now I know that almost everyone has similar feelings about themselves at one time or another. There will always be people who seem to be better than you, and you will always feel stupid, or not as talented as they are, if you compare yourself to them. It is important not to be overtaken by feelings of stupidity, and to accept yourself for the person you are, loved by God and created to live a special life.

Dear Lord, help me to realize that I am not stupid, but instead to know that I am a special person whom You will always care for and love, no matter what. Amen.

My Activities vs. Family Activities

by Gretchen Ricker

Jill was a fun-loving, pretty, fourteen-year-old girl. She got along well with her family; they often went to the lake, and they played games together when they were at home. Her parents took an active interest in her life, and Jill always asked for, and valued, their opinions.

Jill had friends, but she did not spend an excessive amount of time with them. She talked to her friends on the phone sometimes, and went shopping or to the movies with them, but she spent the vast majority of her time doing things with her family. Jill's family was fun to be around. Sometimes her friends came over just to watch television or a movie, and to be around her family.

Then, things changed. Tim became Jill's boyfriend, and suddenly, she was on the phone all the time. When she was not talking on the telephone, she was at Tim's house, or off in her special world, thinking about him. At first her family was glad that she was so happy. After a while though, the phone calls and daydreaming started to get old. Every time that Jill's family wanted to do something together, Jill had something else planned with Tim. She did not have time to talk with her parents; Jill left them out of her life completely.

This separation from her family went on for some time. The relationship between Jill and her parents deteriorated. They stopped asking her to do things with them, and she began to feel left out. When a problem with school or with one of her friends came up, Jill did not feel that she could talk with her parents about it. And, Tim did not have all the answers either!

When Tim broke up with her, Jill sat in her room and cried for a long time. She realized that she did not know what to do at home anymore because she had not done anything with her family for so long.

After she had moped around for a couple of days, Jill's mother asked her if she wanted to go shopping with her. Jill and her mother spent the day shopping. They talked about everything that had happened in their family lately. Jill realized that she had been missing her family. It was a great time, shopping and talking with her mom.

After that day, Jill decided to spend more time with her family. She knew she could not be with them all the time, but she did begin to deliberately make some time for them in her schedule. She was much happier that way, and her family got along much better.

Dear God, help me to be thankful that I have a family that cares about me and wants to do things with me. Help me to enjoy my family. Amen.

Broken Promises

by Melissa Christian

Liz cried when she told me about it. It was the last basketball game of the season and her mother had not come. Her mother had promised all season that she would come to a game and watch Liz play, but for some reason or another she could never make it, not even once. Now Liz wonders if her mother just doesn't care about her.

I've never lived through a situation exactly like Liz's, but my parents have broken promises that they made to me. And it always hurts—no matter how big, or how little, the promise is. Sometimes it makes me wonder if they just don't like me.

Your parents have probably broken promises they made to you. You might even have had an experience like Liz's. Have you ever felt the way she did? I have, and your friends probably have, and even your parents have been hurt when someone made promises to them that were not kept.

When your parents break promises, you may start to feel unloved and unwanted. But remember, sometimes broken promises cannot be avoided. Situations do come up that prevent parents from keeping promises. And sometimes they just forget. The fact is that your parents are not perfect. They are human, just like us, and they make mistakes.

When your parents break a promise, talk to them about your feelings. Don't yell; just tell them that you feel upset or left out. Help them understand how you feel. Also, I think it is important for you to forgive your parents. Remember that they have a lot on their minds and many things to do, and breaking a promise probably does not mean that they love or care for you any less than you thought.

The most important promise ever made to you was the one

God made. He promised that He would send his only Son to earth to live, die for your sins, and then rise from the dead. God kept that promise, and no matter what happens, you can always count on Him to be there for you. He will always love and care for you. And God keeps *all* of His promises!

Dear Lord, please help me to be understanding and forgiving toward my parents when they break their promises. Amen.

God! What Is Wrong with Me?

by Tracey Schramm

Let me tell you about my second day in junior high school. I guess I should have felt excited that I was growing up, but somehow that day I felt like a lost child in an adult world. I sat at lunch by myself and watched others in the lunch room talking and laughing. They were having a good time, and I felt so left out. When lunch was over, I walked into the bathroom and looked into the mirror. I stood there, staring at myself, asking God what was wrong with me. Was it my hair, my body, or that zit in the middle of my forehead? I almost started to cry, but the bell rang, and I knew that I would be late for Miss Johnson's social studies class.

When I got to class, I heard some students making plans for Friday night. I knew that I would be spending the night going out to eat with my parents. Why was this happening to me? Why couldn't I be back at my old school with my old friends?

Somehow I got through my last class and solemnly walked to my bus. I picked the last open seat and stared idly out the window on the long ride home. When I got in the house, I laid down on the couch and cried, until a voice inside of me said to dry up the tears, kneel, and pray to God.

Every Sunday I had sat in church like a zombie, never paying attention to what was said. The people I heard speak about the true Savior did not seem realistic to me, and I did not think that they understood me. Yet, somehow, now I felt this yearning to pray. I knelt down to this wonderful God I had heard about, and I told him all my hopes and fears, and all my sadness. When I was finished I felt that I had a friend I could talk to, a friend who was warm and caring and loving. Here was a friend I could really trust, someone who would never leave me. I felt better right away, and soon I had the determination and confidence I needed to meet the next day.

Now, please do not think that everything turned out totally great just because I prayed. The next day was much the same as before. When I got home I cried a little again, but then I prayed, and I felt better again. The next day at lunch I looked around the room and saw others, sitting alone, just like me. I walked over and began talking to some of them, and we discovered that we had a lot in common. Remember, I did not say that going to a new school and making new friends would be easy, but I did say that when I asked Jesus for His help and His love, He gave me the hope and strength and determination to make those first, difficult steps, and to keep trying.

That day when I knelt and prayed to God was a turning point in my life, a very special day. Now it is two years later, I am in the first weeks of high school, and I still call on the Lord for help every day. I want you to ask the Lord to take you under His protecting wing. Ask Him to show you how to be proud of yourself for what you are and do, so that you can love the person that God has made in you.

Dear God, In all of the rough and lonely times, be with me. Give me the strength to go on, and remind me always to look to you so that I can love the person you are making in me. Amen.

Hand-Me-Downs

by Cori Freudenberg

"I love your outfit," Ashley whispered.

What do I say now—I bought it at the Gap last night? I found it on sale? It belongs to my cousin, and I am just borrowing it?

Finally, I managed to stutter "Oh . . . uh . . . it's only a hand-me-down," and quickly turned my head.

Hand-me-downs! Hand-me-downs were my life! I have about a million older cousins, so I used to live in the clothes that they handed down to me. That is what hand-me-downs are— clothes or jewelry or toys, or sometimes even underwear, handed down from one person to another.

My parents always thought we were so blessed for getting those clothes because my dad works for the church, and we never had money to go out and buy new clothes every year. I, though, hated it! I loathed having to get up every morning and put on old clothes that someone else had worn and then, when they got tired of them or outgrew them, put in a big plastic bag to mail to us.

I always wished I had a cute mini-skirt, or a pair of Guess jeans, or an Esprit top—whatever was in at the moment. How come I was the one who always got the old, used sweater?

Now I am in high school, and guess what? I don't get hand-me-downs anymore! My cousins and I have all stopped growing.

I'm happy now, right? WRONG! I miss those hand-me-downs. I found I loved those jeans that were already broken in and had naturally been given that worn blue jean look. I loved those pajamas that had the corny saying on them. I loved those wild shirts with the big palm trees plastered across the front.

It's fun to buy new clothes, but now that I don't get those hand-me-downs, I wish I had them back. They gave me the chance to experiment and try new outfits without spending a lot of money. And I have noticed that my past is reality for a lot of kids in high school. I think it's neat that kids with hand-me-downs, or dollar clothes from a second-hand shop, sometimes get compliments, just like kids who have a new outfit for every day of the year.

I am not saying that name brands and designer labels are all bad. All I am trying to express is that it is okay to be you, no matter what clothes you have to wear.

You can even be confident enough to start a new trend, or just wear what you want, and be who you want to be. Maybe your clothes don't have designer labels, and maybe your outfit will not always turn out quite the way you expect. That's okay. You have got a whole life to live and find out who you want to be.

Don't feel bad if you do not have brand new clothes. And, if you do have new clothes, don't make those with hand-me-downs feel like they are lesser people. Make clothes a way to show character and your own personality, rather than the size of your parents' checkbook!

Lord, help me to feel confident enough about myself so that I do not need designer labels to feel like a somebody. And, Lord, if you have a chance, could you send me some more hand-me-downs? Amen.

"It's me. It's definitely me."

When Your Best Isn't Good Enough

by Susan Van Dermeulen

I'm trying so hard. How come nobody notices me? There is always somebody better than I am. That person makes what I do look like junk. I try my best, but I can never be on top. Instead, I am always pushed into the crowd. Why won't anyone notice me? What I do is important too! Why should I try if nobody cares? It's not worth it.

Many people begin to think like this when they feel that their best is not good enough. Whether it is a talent they have that is not recognized, or they feel that they have not been recognized as a person by others, they feel inferior and left out.

I felt this way many times. When I started a new school and no one knew me, I felt so hopeless. I studied hard every night, but I never seemed to know the right answer in class. In sports, I tried so hard so I would be noticed by the coaches. All I needed to hear was, "I know you, you're so-and-so," or "Nice play, keep it up." Just something, so that I knew I really mattered to someone. But those positive responses never came.

1 John 3:1–2 has really helped me in times like this: "How great is the love the Father has lavished on us, that we should be called children of God! And that is what we are! The reason the world does not know us is that it did not know Him. Dear friends, now we are children of God, and what we will be has not yet been made known. But we know that when He appears, we shall be like Him, for we shall see Him as He is."

To me that means that even though I might not get the compliments or the recognition that I want, I am very special. God has made me specially, and he loves me unconditionally.

You and I are children of God, and that is the most important family of all. So when we give our best, we cannot worry if others seem to expect more of us. God knows that we are trying hard, and that we need love, and He loves us and accepts us. He will recognize us, and remind us how very extraordinary we really are.

Dear Lord, Please grant me the strength to do everything to the best of my ability, even though it may not seem to be the best to someone else. Help me to remember that I am special, and thank You for making me Your child. Amen.

What Happened to My Time?

by Angie Tuerck

Pop quiz?

The class was in an uproar following Miss Lenden's announcement of a surprise quiz on last night's history assignment. Billy saw Amie glance at him with a look of fear. He knew that she, too, had not had time to complete the homework.

The past few weeks had been unusually busy for Billy, Amie, and other seventh graders. Amie and Billy had the lead roles in the school play, and they both had spent hours learning their lines. The dress rehearsal last night had left no time for homework.

After doing their best to make educated guesses on the quiz, Amie and Billy met at their lockers. "Why don't we try and go over our lines one more time before the opening tonight?" Billy suggested.

"Sure," Amie answered. "How about right now?"

"No," Billy shook his head. "I have soccer tryouts. Can we do it after that?"

"That won't work," Amie said. "I have a piano lesson and then come straight back to school for make-up. I guess we'll have to go with what we've got. Let's hope we can do all right."

"Okay, we'll see what we can do. I have to go. Oh, would you maybe want to go out for some ice cream or something after the show tonight?"

"Billy, that would be fun. But I already promised my family I'd go out with them. I'm sorry. Maybe some other time?"

"Yeah, sure," Billy said. As he walked to soccer tryouts he kept thinking of how he rarely had any time to do the things he really wanted to do. He missed playing baseball with his neighborhood buddies. And now that he was in the play, there was even less time than before. What happened to *my* time and *my* fun? Billy wondered.

When Billy's mom picked him up after soccer tryouts, he told her about not being ready for the history quiz.

"Why weren't you ready?" Mom asked.

"I don't know, Mom. It's just that things are so busy now. I had soccer practice after school yesterday, and then the dress rehearsal. There was no time to read history. There are so many things going on, I just don't know what to do anymore."

"Why don't you sit down for a while this weekend and sort out your activities? Write down the things that are most important to you. I might suggest putting homework first on the list," Mom smiled. "Then list as many other things as you think you can handle."

"Yeah, that sounds like a plan," Billy agreed. "Say, Mom? Could our family maybe go out for ice cream after the show tonight? I know the perfect place."

Dear Lord, thank You for blessing me with many talents. Help me to realize what is most important to me and to manage my time in a way that is pleasing to You. Amen.

*"How about getting together after the soccer
game and your piano lesson, before play
practice and after the library closes?"*

Nine O'Clock?

by Noel Reisdorf

Judy slammed the car door. She sat in the back seat with tears rolling down her cheeks. She looked out of the window at her friends, laughing and joking around. She then looked at her father solemnly getting into the driver's seat.

"I could have stayed longer, you know," Judy hissed.

"Well, there will be other times," her father said, as though he did not care.

No, there would not be another time, Judy thought. She had had Joey right where she wanted him. He had opened his mouth, and Judy was sure that it was to ask her the question that would have changed her whole life. Then her dad pulled up, honking the horn, reminding her of her 9:00 curfew, almost like he had planned it. Everyone else had a 9:30 or a 10:00 curfew. Not her though, her parents would not let her do anything without a contract written in blood.

"Why couldn't I stay longer?" Judy asked as they pulled into their driveway.

"Judy, we have gone over this before. You can't stay out past 9:00 until you're in high school." Her father was impatient. Judy pouted the whole way home.

Judy slammed the bedroom door behind her and cried some more. Why didn't they trust her? Why was she treated like such a kid? It was not like she would have done anything really bad. Judy stroked her purring cat.

"You trust me, don't you, Kitty?" Judy cooed. The cat squinted its eyes in agreement.

Judy heard a knock at her door, and ignored it. Her mother stepped in anyway.

"Judy, I heard that you did not appreciate your father picking you up."

"Huh," Judy grunted.

"Why is that?" her mother prodded.

"Why don't you trust me?" Judy was close to tears.

"It's not that we don't trust you, dear, it is just that the mall closes at eight. What are you going to do after that?"

"There are other places, Mom. We could go to someone's house or something."

"Well, that's just it. If you did that, I wouldn't know where you were in case I needed to get hold of you."

"Mom, telephones were invented for a reason," Judy snapped.

"Please, don't get smart with me. We don't need that to settle this. Now, maybe we can work out a calling system, and you could call before you go somewhere different."

"Mom," Judy whined.

"Judy, freedom doesn't happen just like that!" Mom snapped her fingers. "You have to earn it, little by little. Think about it."

As Judy's mom shut the door, Judy began to think about it.

When she got ready for bed she prayed, "Dear Lord, please help me to be responsible and gain more of my parents' trust. Amen."

Feeling calmer, she laid down, and fell into a deep sleep.

Dear God, help my parents understand how much I need a little extra freedom. And help me remember how much they love me. Amen.

Why Does God Let Bad Things Happen to Me?

by Matt Peterman

"Let my people go!" shouted Moses, as he led the children of Israel out of captivity in Egypt. The children of Israel must have wondered why these bad times were upon them. They even thought God was the cause.

- Why is Mom an alcoholic?
- Why did God let my dog die?
- How could God let me make such a fool of myself?
- Why did God make me unattractive?
- Why must God always let me be sick?
- How come God let my parents get a divorce?
- Why didn't God let my team win?

Before you decide that God is the cause and reason for the things that you feel are bad, you might want to consider this: God is your creator and loves you very much. Many times you have heard of God's *grace*. It means God's *undeserved love*, and it's true. God loves you no matter what you do, and He proved it by putting His Son on the cross to die for you.

Evil and sin are bad things. God does not punish you for each wrong, and He never deliberately makes bad things happen to you. As long as there is sin in this world, bad things and evil-acting people will exist. Our sin, the sins of other people, and the work of Satan are the reasons for bad things, not God.

Have you ever heard anyone say, "Suffering builds character?" It may seem inappropriate, even cruel at times, but there is some truth in it. Ask God to help you when you're in trouble. He will strengthen you and build you up so you can face problems. You can share your experiences with others who have troubles and help comfort them.

Paul says, "And we know that in all things God works for the good of those who love Him" (Rom. 8:28). God loves you and is working for your good. To "love" God in return doesn't have anything to do with romantic love. It means having faith in Him and trusting Him to do what's best for you.

When you start to shout with the children of Israel, remember how God led them out of slavery and brought them to a beautiful home. Have faith in God. Don't let evil and sin get in the way of your receiving God's grace and forgiveness. He will work everything out for your good.

Dear God, help me to remember that I must have Your courage to live in a world of sin and evil. Comfort me by reminding me that You are with me, helping me to understand my problems and live with joy. Amen.

My Church Is Different from Your Church

by Jennifer McCain

"You haven't been baptized, so you're going to hell!" Mia proclaimed to Loretta.

"I will get baptized when I get older, just like Jesus was," Loretta shot back, obviously hurt and offended.

I couldn't believe my ears. The three of us had been going to school together since kindergarten, and here Mia and Loretta were arguing over heaven and hell.

Many young people are confused and worried because of the differences in the many Christian churches. Some of us argue to defend our specific denomination, but end up wondering who is really right. It is a scary experience that can bewilder a person.

It is important to look for similarities between the denominations of the Christian faith. Hopefully, the most important one is that we believe in Jesus our Savior. We believe that the Holy Spirit works faith in believers' hearts. God's Word says, "You are all sons of God through faith in Jesus Christ" (Gal. 3:26). We experience feelings of joy and thanksgiving because Jesus' death and resurrection mean that our sins are forgiven.

The differences between denominations have caused numerous controversies throughout history, and still cause problems today. Where do denominations come from? Denominations were established by men, not by God.

There are some points in the Bible that are not crystal clear to sinful man. Because of these uncertainties, people and churches have established their own interpretations. The differences in them can vary from when a person should be baptized, to whether to use wine or grape juice for communion.

Since it is important to know and believe what the Bible says, these differences are significant. But, they should not be stumbling blocks in our relationships with each other. Discussing them should be a fun and enlightening experience, not something that causes us to dislike each other. Celebrating our oneness in Christ is best, but we must understand that the differences will be around until Jesus comes again, and sometimes we may have to disagree.

Dear Lord, help me to be faithful to Your Word and Your truth. Help me to be kind when I talk to friends who believe differently. And help me be ready to explain my faith in You. Amen.

Is God Really There?

by Alison Witbrodt

I could have gotten hurt a lot worse than I did. Was it luck, or did God have a protective hand in my life?

I walked in the door of Meghan's house. Her little brothers were having a birthday party, and she asked me to come and keep her company.

We decided to go on a bike ride, and since I had forgotten my bike, I borrowed Meghan's old one. Little did I know that the blue bike's brakes did not always work!

Meghan led the way to the top of an enormous hill. At the bottom of the hill, I saw a dry creek bed with plenty of rocks and no fence around it. The road ran dead end into another road which crossed it right before the creek.

I love riding bikes, so when I saw the hill I took off down it like a flash! About halfway down the hill, I decided I ought to slow down, so I put on the brakes. Only I did not slow down, I kept going faster! The brakes were not working!

Just before the creek there was a strip of grass. I decided to try to jump off my bike and onto the grass since I could not turn or stop. I jumped. Would I land on the grass or in the creek?

I landed in the creek. Thankfully the bike landed next to me—right next to me as a matter of fact—not on me. At first I could not move. It was just shock, but I thought I was paralyzed or something! Meghan peered over the edge asking all sorts of questions. To this day I do not remember what they were.

She helped me out of the water, and we walked back to her house. I had a bump the size of a goose egg on my head, and my right leg rapidly turned a sickly shade of purple, but otherwise, I was okay.

Was it luck I did not get hurt worse, or was God acting in

my life? At the time I did not think about it, but later the thought flew through my head.

Doubt. That is the word. Was I doubting God? The thought horrified me! Did that mean I was not a good Christian, or that I had a weak faith? I struggled with it for a while, but as I talked to people and prayed, God brought me to a conclusion.

Doubting is part of building faith, not a terrible thing to ignore. If I would not have come to a decision on my doubt and ignored it instead, then it could have caused trouble. But I confronted my doubt and stared it in the face; and I learned from it and grew in my faith.

A friend once told me that God only allows bad things to happen to you if you can handle it. Whenever you have a problem, you can know that God is right there with you, helping you.

So, when I doubt God or His ways, it's okay. I just take some time out, confront my doubt, talk about it to a friend or someone I can trust, and pray. God promises to hear me and help me.

I hope that you will come to the same conclusion I did. God did have a hand in my life, and He still does each and every day.

Dear Lord, when I doubt You and struggle with my faith, help me to remember You are watching over me. Amen.

Measuring Up . . .
What Do They Want from Me?

by Elizabeth Strubbe

Jennifer came home with a C – on an important test. At least her parents thought it was important—she could care less about science! Jenni really wanted to be an interior decorator. She was proud that her room always looked very modern and was decorated tastefully. Her friends all thought that she would be a great decorator, too, but somehow her parents did not understand her wish. Jenni wanted to please her parents, but at the same time she did not want to be doing something that would make her miserable for the rest of her life.

Often parents have their own ideas about what their child should do and be, but their child has a very different idea. Is it wrong to have a different goal in mind than the one your parents have for you? Think of Jesus, the most obedient child who ever lived. He stayed behind at the temple in Jerusalem while His parents returned home. He knew He had other work to do!

We are not Jesus, and our future is not exactly like His future, but we do have Jesus' example. So we can do with our lives what we feel God wants us to do. We will have to carefully listen to our parents, consider their hopes and ideas, and then make our decision, even if it is not exactly what our parents think that we should do.

Parents and children both make mistakes. That should not shock anyone. Parents mess up when they try to force their ideas on their children; and children mess up when they angrily get fed up with their parents' expectations. But messing up is definitely forgivable! And agreeing on a career is not an impossible problem either!

It is important to talk with your parents about the things you want to do, and what you want to become. Your parents may not realize that they have been putting pressure on you, and they should hear what you want to do, so that they can support you in your choice of a career.

Dear God, thank You for my parents, even though we sometimes disagree. Give me Your help in choosing a career that is pleasing to You. Amen.

*"Mom, Dad, instead of becoming a doctor, I've decided
to become an underwater demolitions expert."*

No One Is Listening

by Lauren Weinhold

"Mom, you'll never guess what kind of a day I had!"

"Not now, honey, I have lots of errands to run."

"Dad?"

"Shhh! Can't you see, I'm trying to watch the game!"

"Hey Erin, guess what?"

"Can't you see I'm on the phone? I have to find out where Julie got her outfit."

Do these conversations sound familiar? If they do, you are not alone! As teenagers we are quite often faced with problems or worries that never seemed like a big deal when we were nine or ten years old. We may also feel the need to pour our heart out to a friend, parent, or yes, even that ragged teddy bear slumped on our bed. And sometimes the teddy bear is the best listener because it has no meetings or volleyball practices to attend.

But do not become discouraged. Even at our worst moments, when it seems as if no wants to listen and no one really cares, just remember that God is a light at the end of the tunnel. God is always there to listen to us, and help us through those days when we are at our worst!

And even though this may be hard to believe, friends and family do genuinely care about us, and want to listen to our troubles. But, just like all of us do at one time or another, they become caught up in something that is for the moment "more important."

Maybe you are accused of this sometimes too. You see, being listened to is no more important than being a listener yourself.

I recall an afternoon when a friend of mine called me and told me that she was having problems at home. Before she could continue, I blurted out that I had to go outside to get a tan before the sun went down. She said "okay" and hung up. About five minutes later I called her back, remembering a time when she had been there for me. Let's face it, I felt like a fool. I had just broken my best friend's heart so I could go out and lay in the sun. Can you see what is wrong with this picture?

We all know the verse, "So in everything, do to others what you would have them do to you," which we call the Golden Rule. It is from the Bible and it makes good sense. I know I discovered that day, that in order to be listened to, I must be willing to listen. All you need are two ears and a willing heart.

Dear Lord, help me to know that You are always there to listen to me. Let me be willing to listen to others also. In Jesus' name. Amen.

My Best Friend Isn't

by Christine Hawkins

Having a best friend is great! Overnights, movies, long phone conversations, and studying together; do these sound familiar? Fun times like these will always be remembered. But what happens when a friendship fizzles? When the relationship ends with an argument, or a misunderstanding, the feelings that one has are very upsetting.

Why did the friendship end? Maybe the two people involved just grew apart. This is a common reason that friendships stop. People can grow up differently and have a different set of values, views, and beliefs. Sometimes these differences can get in the way. Maybe the friends do not have the same schedules, or no longer do the same activity, such as a sport or a hobby. Since they do not spend as much time together as they did before, it is hard to stay close.

However, at times the thing that ends friendships is jealousy. Two friends can become jealous over many things. Now, it might be something minor, like clothes, or something major, like who gets more dates. Remember, God gives us all gifts, but not the same gifts to all. Look at yourself, do not worry about others, and develop the gifts that God has given to you.

Another thing that can affect a friendship is competition. When a common interest that draws friends together becomes too competitive, it can also push them apart. Friends can overcome this dilemma by working together, instead of being rivals.

If two friends just cannot get along, it may be okay to let the "best friends" relationship end. But the two could still be friends. They could still say "hi" in the halls and help each other with homework.

Remember, as you move through life you will make many

acquaintances. Your set of friends will change as you progress on through high school, college, and beyond. So don't be upset by the fact that you are not as close to a certain friend as you used to be, because you will always have joyful memories of your experiences as you move on to new friends.

Jesus, help me to see that friends are blessings, and that each new friend is a new blessing. Amen.

Betrayal

by Ryan Ricker

Picture this: Nate and Michael were in their last year of junior high school. They were popular and out-going boys. So, it was only natural that these two would become friends. Eventually they grew to be best friends; very rarely was one seen without the other.

There was, though, an underlying difference in their home lives. Nate and his parents did everything that a healthy family does together. Michael came from a broken home, and his family did almost nothing together. He did not even know who his biological father was until he was eight years old.

Nate and Michael did many crazy things together during the year. They told each other secrets that they would not have dared to tell anyone else. Michael formed a bond with Nate's parents too. Unfortunately, Nate did not understand this. Nate, who had grown up with loving parents, did not realize that Michael's parents were hardly ever home, and that he really needed this attachment with caring adults. Michael even took a ski trip with Nate and his parents that winter, and the two boys had a great time together. These were dudes who knew how to have fun on the slopes. Michael enjoyed his time in the mountains with Nate's parents.

Trouble erupted that spring. On the night of the high school prom, Michael slashed some car tires. Those who knew him well felt that this was simply a cry for his parents' attention. Two policemen arrested him at school, and they questioned Nate too. Everyone suspected that Nate was also involved because of his relationship with Michael.

Nate was frightened. He was already in trouble with his parents because of other things he had done with Michael in the past few months, like sneaking out of the house, and drinking. Nate had done these things in an effort to "prove himself" to Michael and their friends, but he did have Christian parents who had taught and guided him in setting better values.

Finally, Nate abandoned his best friend because of fear. He could have asked his parents for help, or worked it out one-on-one with Michael. Instead, he gave up, and they both lost what might have been the best friendship either of them would ever have.

Thankfully the tire slashing was the last instance of law breaking for Michael. But whenever I think about Michael and Nate, I think about my own close friends. I ask God to give me the courage to stick both by my friends and my Christian values. And I think about my parents. I want to be open enough with them that I can go to them whenever I—or one of my friends— have a problem.

Dear God, I know that You are the creator of friendship. Help me to give my friend the same forgiveness and understanding that You have given to me. Amen.

Different-colored Friends

by Ryan Smith

I see them walking down the hallway together. They congregate in one part of each classroom. I walk down the hallway, and I feel uncomfortable as I pass through the area that seems to be their hangout. I feel a sense of separation at all of these times. I perceive that I am not wanted. As I think about it, it is obvious that I do not want much to do with them either. Come on, think about it; their skin color, their language, and their dress are nothing like mine. Why would I want to become friends with any of them?

Boy, what a fool I was when I thought like that! I almost used my misguided beliefs in stereotypes to cheat myself out of many valuable friendships, because I only saw the differences between us.

One day, something happened that began to change my opinion. John was one of "them," and his locker was next to my locker in the locker room. One day after practice he picked up my watch for me. It most likely would have been stolen, because that had happened before. He kept it in his locker overnight, and gave it back to me at school the next day.

Another incident, on the football field, changed the way I had thought about him. I saw John slip and fall, and it was one of the worst tumbles I had ever seen. My heart went out to him as he rolled on the muddy field. I helped to carry him to the parking lot, and I stayed with him until the ambulance came. While we were waiting, I tried to help him keep his mind off his pain. We talked about the same things that I usually talked about with my friends. I made a friend that day, and we have been talking about what friends talk about every day since.

So, these two discoveries changed my attitude about John

forever. I realized that he was a compassionate and feeling person, just like me; and, that he was a person I wanted to be friends with.

When I look back to then, it is hard to believe that I was so ignorant. How could I have been so shallow as to think that the color of someone's skin should determine whether or not he could be my friend? The things that are really important are characteristics that everybody can have, like compassion, caring, and loyalty.

Jesus, thank You for making me like, and different from, everybody else, and help me to realize that it is what is underneath that counts, and not the color of my skin. Amen.

Defending David

by Liz Hellstern

My stomach started going flip-flop when I saw the bus coming toward us. Why, oh, why can't Mom take us to school? I hate riding the bus.

My younger brother and I got on. David sat in the only empty seat. I pretended that I didn't know him, and walked to the back where all my friends were.

That's when all the trouble started. Some of the older boys began making fun of David. That's why I hated riding the bus. Every day they found some new way to hurt him. You're probably wondering what's wrong with David. Not a thing! He's just a little kid, easy to pick on. I felt sorry for him, but I was always so embarrassed! I found myself keeping quiet. If I'd had enough guts, I would have told those bullies to leave him alone.

After school, we went home and found the house empty. "I guess Mom must still be at work. We should really start supper if we want to eat tonight," I said.

David silently helped me peel potatoes. Finally he asked me, "Liz, why does everybody hate me?"

After trying to make David feel better, I retreated to my room. I turned on the stereo immediately to drown out my feelings. But no matter how loud I made it, my thoughts still bothered me. I finally had to face the fact that I wasn't much better in my behavior toward David than the bullies. But, I knew that I loved him, so I resolved to do something to show him that. But what?

That night I didn't sleep very well. I kept trying to find ways out of my resolve. Just as I was drifting off to sleep, I thought of the time David had given me earrings for Christmas. He had scrimped and saved for that present, and was so proud when I opened it. I thought of when we were younger and acted like best friends. He even let me dress him up as a little girl! I knew what I had to do.

Morning finally came and we waited for the bus. David wasn't looking forward to the ride, I could tell. He walked up the steps and sat in his usual seat. I hesitated, and then sat down next to him. David looked up at me. His smile was worth everything.

Dear Lord, Let me remember that my family is a gift from You, even though they sometimes seem like blessings in disguise. Amen.

Church Burnout

by Brian Feidler

Saturday night was so great! I came in and got to bed around 1:00 A.M. But a few hours later I had to get up and go to church.

I was sick of getting up early and going to church and Sunday school every Sunday morning. It was the same old thing, every week. After seven or eight years of going to Sunday school, I had heard all of the Bible stories. I knew all about God and the cool things that Jesus did on this earth. Did they think that I would suddenly forget them or something? After a while, I turned it all off. I was not the only one who felt this way. I knew people that read the bulletin during the sermon or talked to a friend during Sunday school. And some of my friends don't go to church or Sunday school at all anymore.

But once I got to church, I started doing some thinking. As time passes, a person could forget things you thought you would never forget—like the Lord's Prayer and simple Bible passages that you used to just rattle off. Finally, you could begin to lose sight of God and what He means to you.

Church may seem boring at times, and the hymns a bit out of date. You might talk to your pastor or youth worker about planning a youth Sunday once in a while. Young people can choose songs, play instruments, and serve as ushers and readers. Becoming involved really helps!

Being part of a youth group or helping start a youth ministry is also a great way to get involved and have fun in the church. Typically, activities in youth ministry range from going out together for pizza to going on weekend trips, or longer trips to youth gatherings. At events like these, young people get together to learn and grow. It is all fun, and experiences are planned to help strengthen your faith. There may be other youth ministry activities, too, like service projects for homeless or helpless people, study and prayer groups, or sports teams.

Try listening to the sermon too. It may be hard to believe, but some of what the pastor says applies to you right now! Ask your Sunday school teacher or youth worker if you can deal with some of the issues you face—drugs, dating, alcohol, premarital sex—in Bible class. Taking an active part in your church will keep you interested in attending.

When your schedule gets busy, it is good to sit down for an hour or two to think about how God works in your life and how you are responding to Him. It is really relaxing to know that in our world, there is always one place to go when the going is rough—God's house. Try it!

Dear Lord, please help me not to burn out on church. Help me to get the most out of worship as I hear, learn, and share Your Word. Amen.

Two Choices at Curfew

by Jill Miller

Sweat beaded in the palms of my hands and my heart took off in a frenzy as the boy I had had a crush on since the fourth grade asked me to dance. It was my first junior high dance. I had waited all night for this moment to come. Then I glanced at the clock. It was 10:56; my curfew was 11:00. Two choices remained. Number 1: Give up the chance to dance with him and obey the rule Mom and Dad had made, or, Number 2: Take the golden opportunity to dance with this guy and risk being grounded. Of course I danced with the boy. It was a stupid rule anyway, I decided.

When I arrived at my house fifteen minutes late, my parents were seated side by side in chairs across from the door.

"I know I'm late, and I'm sorry. Eric finally asked me to dance, and I couldn't turn him down!" I stuttered quickly, "It'll never happen again."

My parents seemed not to hear a word I had said. They just sat and stared. Finally my dad spoke up, "Go to bed. We'll talk tomorrow morning." I was so relieved; they did not punish me.

The next morning, Mom sat me down and explained that rules are made for my own benefit. When I started to think about it, I finally understood. If Mom and Dad did not care about me, I might be able to stay out until 1:00. But, because they love me and care about my well-being, I have rules. They are only trying to protect me from getting hurt. I guess 11:00 isn't bad after all, I thought to myself, and at least they care!

Dear God, help me to obey the rules my parents make for me, and help me to understand that they make rules because they care about me. Amen.

Communicating— the Big Struggle

by Allison Oehlert

Sarah talked to me with tears rolling down her face. She had had another fight with her parents. It seemed that no matter how hard they tried, Sarah and her parents had trouble communicating. Almost every time Sarah came home from school, she or her parents would start in with the yelling.

Sarah felt that no one was listening. She was afraid to tell her parents when she got a bad grade on a test or an assignment. She hated to let them down, and start the arguing and yelling again.

In all families there is some faulty communication. Sharing and listening takes time and effort. Explaining what you mean and how you feel is often difficult.

Many arguments in my family could have been avoided. Instead of trying to solve a little disagreement, we often let it build to something larger. I always wanted to use the excuse that my parents were not listening to me. Some of the time that might have been true, but I was not always listening to them either. Wanting to believe I was right, and they were wrong, was a basic communication breakdown. Sometimes I wish I would have just listened to them and then, perhaps, they would have listened to me.

My mom would always ask me about my day at school and if anything went wrong. I usually said everything was fine or okay, and I did not realize that Mom was sending me an invitation to talk to her about her feelings too. She eventually made me realize that I never asked her how she was. After that I tried to remember to show concern for my parents' day. It made a big difference.

Communication will always be a problem. My parents had trouble talking with their parents. You can expect to go through some hard times. You may have a dreadful day at school and take it out on your parents. I have done that. And your parents will probably do it to you too.

But, think about talking with your parents as a give-and-take relationship. Sometimes it might need to be more giving on your part. There are times you just have to realize that it is not fair to impose your frustrations on your parents. It is best to talk things out calmly with them. They just may understand.

A Bible passage that helps me is Ephesians 6:1–3. "Children, obey your parents in the Lord, for this is right. 'Honor your father and mother'—which is the first commandment with a promise— 'that it may go well with you and that you may enjoy long life on the earth.' " The next verse has helped my family too. "Fathers, do not exasperate your children; instead, bring them up in the training and instruction of the Lord" (Eph. 6:4).

That talks about the way the relationship between parents and children should be in God's eyes. It has helped my family sometimes to just sit back and listen to each other.

Dear Heavenly Father, help me to always remember You are the best listener. Guide me to know when to listen and when to share with my family. In Jesus' name. Amen.

"How was your day, Mom? Would you
like some milk and cookies?"

How Can I Make More Friends?

by Sara Goetzke and Kristin Ricker

Dear Rudy:

I just moved to a new town, and I have always had problems making friends because I am too shy. How should I go about making new friends?

Friendless

Dear Friendless:

Lots of people have problems making friends because they are too shy. Try to be more outgoing, and talk to people more. A good way to start a conversation is to ask people questions about themselves. Invite people to go somewhere with you, instead of waiting for them to ask you. Remember, to have a friend you must be a friend. Another thing to remember is to always be yourself and greet everyone with a smile.

Rudy

Dear Rudy:

My mom always told me to choose my friends wisely. I am not sure what I should be looking for. Please help.

Still Friendless

Dear Friendless:

It really depends on what *you* want in a friend. That's probably what your mom meant. There are basic things you should look for. For example, friends should have some of the same interests you enjoy, and you should feel comfortable being around them. They should be able to listen to your problems and make you feel good about yourself (like you do for them).

Rudy

Dear Rudy:

I do not have much of a problem making friends now; it is just keeping them that is hard. What am I doing wrong?

Friendless Once Again

Dear Friendless:

It is hard to say that you are doing something wrong. Some people think of themselves first, instead of their friends. To find out if this is your problem, examine how you treat your friends. See if this is how you would like them to treat you.

Rudy

Hopefully, answering these questions that people your age often ask will help you in the future when it comes to looking for, making, and keeping friends.

Dear God, please help me to choose good friends and to be a good friend to others. Amen.

Mom and Dad Are Old Fogies

by Jill Miller

From the day I was born, my parents have been there for me at everything I do. Deep down inside I am glad they are there. I have, though, been in a situation when I just wanted to say, "Whose parents are they? I'm glad they aren't mine."

Picture this scene at a basketball game. Dad promised he would be there, like always. I had not seen him yet, and it was already the second half. Then it happened. Out of the corner of my eye I saw him standing in the middle of the doorway. I almost passed out from embarrassment right in the middle of the court.

"Is that your dad?" a teammate asked.

"I'm not sure," I replied as my face turned cherry red. Let me explain why I was embarrassed. On Dad's feet were the black and white loafers my grandma had given him back in the Dark Ages. He wore blue, red, and white plaid and, I repeat, *plaid*, pants with a shirt he considered to be "coordinating." To top off his ensemble, a cowboy hat sat on top of his head. (Now you know why Mom gets up ten minutes early to get Dad dressed).

Well, he came to see me play, and I was glad for that. I am certain that you have been in my shoes at some point in your life. Sometimes you would just like to take your parents aside and ask, "Is this what they taught you in school? Please, grow out of it," but they would probably ground you for such remarks.

Anyway, here are four quick ways to overcome embarrassing parents:

1. Turn around, smile, and say, "I was adopted."
2. Hold up a sign with these words, "Parents 4 sale. CHEAP."
3. Pretend not to see them. When someone asks about them reply, "Who? What? Where?"

4. Just keep in mind that everyone has parents who are sometimes "old fogies" too.

By the way, Dad, remember I love you no matter what you decide to wear!

Dear God, thank You for giving me parents to love me. Although things are sometimes not like I want them to be, remind me how much they do for me. In Jesus' name. Amen.

"I've never seen that man in my life."

My Prayer Line

by Christina Boos

I watched as the police car pulled out of my driveway and drove down the street. All I could do now was wait. I walked over to the phone and looked at it, as if my stare could make it ring. I sat next to it, and once again reflected on all that had happened.

I remembered walking home from school, just like we always did. Then a car engine rumbled behind us and, as we turned to see what it was, a truck swerved and hit my friend Jamie square in the back. The events that followed happened so fast that it's hard to believe they could have been real—the police, the sirens, the questions from the detective. I could still see them putting Jamie into the ambulance, and I could still hear his screams of pain as they drove away.

R-I-I-I-NG! The piercing ringing of the telephone interrupted my thoughts. I lunged at the phone in hopes that it might be information about Jamie's condition. I pushed the receiver to my ear, my hand shaking all the way.

I had barely uttered a hello, when I heard a computer's voice sing, "This is a survey for a local research company and we'd . . . " I slammed down the phone and wondered how a device that had given me so much joy could betray me. I thought about all of the times I had talked to Jamie on the phone. I wanted so much for him to call me.

My mom walked in the room. "He'll be okay," she said. "God is with him." Then she left.

That one sentence said more to me than any other sentence that I had ever heard in my whole life. At that moment I decided to call God, on my own personal line, through prayer. I asked God to be with Jamie, and I asked Him to hold him in His healing arms. I asked God to be with all of us who care about Jamie, and I asked Him to give us an extra measure of the Holy Spirit so that we could be patient, and wait until news of Jamie's condition had a chance to reach us. The minute I said "Amen," the phone rang. The voice on the other end breathed out six words, "He is going to be okay."

Jamie returned to school about a month later, just as happy and healthy as always. To most of those who were affected by the accident, it was history. The case of Jamie's experience may have been closed, but the phone line between me and God would always remain open.

Dear God, thank You for Your gift of prayer. Help me always to keep my phone line to You open. Amen.

Rejection

by Blake Sims

After graduating from high school, Mark Turgeon went to the University of Kansas basketball coach, Larry Brown, and told him that he would be the best point guard he had ever coached. Initially, Coach Brown rejected him. Mark kept trying, however, and he eventually made the team. He worked hard to overcome Coach Brown's rejection, and eventually he became a starting point guard for the Jayhawks. Mark continued his diligent efforts, and in his senior season, he was a key member of the Jayhawks' national championship team.

Rejection is something we must all live with throughout our lives. Even as I am writing this, I realize that I may be rejected. There is no magic solution that will make rejection simply vanish. If, however, we are to become functioning, productive members of society, we must learn to deal positively with rejection.

I can remember several examples of being rejected. One form of rejection came about very quickly as I entered junior high school in seventh grade. I had been fairly popular at grade school. I was not, by any means, the most popular kid in the school, but at least I was not a geek or anything. Since we did not receive letter grades at my school, all anybody knew was that I was one of the "smart kids." As I tried to break into the elite group of popular kids, it became apparent to me that, in some cases, getting good grades, or even caring about school, was looked down upon. Grades simply were not important to the popular group.

Another area of rejection came through sports. Football was the first sport offered in seventh grade. I went out, and since there were no cuts in seventh grade, I made the team. I eventually became first string wide receiver. The quarterback was the unofficial leader of one of the most popular groups in school. Since I was not in his group, he did not pass me the ball very often. I took this as rejection.

A similar situation evolved during basketball season. I was starting on the B Team, and none of the other players particularly liked me. They passed the ball to me as a last resort. This did not feel very good.

Overcoming these feelings was not easy, but I knew God would help me handle it. I knew He had given me athletic ability, and I was finally able to use it to the fullest on the tennis court.

As far as the school situation was concerned, I realized that making good grades was more important than making new friends that might get me into trouble anyway. I realized my old friends from grade school, who already accepted me, were a great blessing. Eventually, I made new friends that were just as concerned about grades as I was.

Mark Turgeon and I have at least one thing in common— we both overcame feelings of rejection in sports by using our God-given talents. Mark was able to fulfill a dream of becoming a Kansas Jayhawk.

When you feel rejected, keep looking to other people or activities as positive support. And remember that you can look to God for your most positive support.

Lord, help me to see that in You I have a friend who will never reject me. Amen.

My Best Friend Moved

by Jennifer McCain

"My dad just gave me the worst news of my entire life!" Pat barely managed to choke out the words. Her face was streaked with tears.

"What? What is it?" I asked, almost not wanting to hear the answer.

"I'm moving to Los Angeles in a couple of weeks . . . " Pat went on to say how her father had been transferred and told me some other details about their move. I was not listening very well, though. I just stood there in disbelief at what I had heard. How could this be happening to me? Pat and I had been best friends since fourth grade; now I was on the verge of being abandoned. What would I do without Pat?

I went through this experience about a year ago. If your best friend tells you that he or she is going to move, you may feel distraught too. Within the first five minutes of knowing, resentment sets in. When Pat told me, all I could think about was how terrible life would be without the one person that I told my deepest secrets to.

Getting past your resentment at a time like this is critical. It is also important to realize that the time you do have left with your friend should be cherished and enjoyed. Spend as much time together as possible.

Saying good-bye is the worst time. Do not feel bad if you do not know what to say; I didn't. Even if I would have known, I would never have been able to get it out through the tears.

I thought that the best way to express to Pat the way I really felt about our friendship was on paper. I wrote her a letter reminiscing about the past, and I told her my hopes for our future together as pen pals. This seemed to work really well for the both of us.

After Pat moved, the reality did not set in until a few days later. I had just heard some exciting gossip. Without even thinking, I called 963-5479, a number I had dialed more times than I would like to think about. I was expecting to hear Pat's cheery "hello" that I was so accustomed to hearing. Instead, I got a recording of an operator's voice. That voice cut into me like a knife. I hung up the phone before the recording was finished. I went up to my room and cried.

I once heard the saying, "Whenever God closes a door, somewhere He opens a window." Well, my life was definitely in God's hands then. And He opened a window in math class, of all places.

Our teacher asked us at the beginning of each math class to discuss our homework with the partner we had chosen at the beginning of the year. Of course, Pat and I were partners, so I never really noticed anyone else in the class, including the girl who sat right behind me. She seemed shy and sort of the "odd number" in class. She had trouble with her assignments and our teacher helped her with her work every day.

Since Pat was gone, I was assigned to be Eileen's partner. I did not think I would enjoy that, so at first I just tried to get our work done as quickly as possible. After a while though, I began to know Eileen. I discovered that she was a very nice person, and that we were very compatible. Eileen became a good friend, and we still are friends today.

As for Pat, we gradually grew apart. It is sad, but in a way, fitting, because life, especially when we are young, is full of changes. Relationships begin, grow, and end, whether someone actually moves away or not. The experience of my friend moving is one I hold close as a time of realization in my life.

Jesus, You are my friend forever. Send friends into my life to fill the emptiness when other friends leave. Amen.

Extremes—Anger and Love, Highs and Lows

by Christine Hawkins

Have you ever been so happy that your cheeks hurt from smiling? Have you ever awakened on time, gotten an A on an English test, and had your mom give you money willingly—all in the same day? It would be great if days were always that good, but, unfortunately, everyone has bad days too.

Sometimes you have days when absolutely everything that could go wrong does. Your teacher yells at you, your mom yells at you, even your grandma gets upset with you. On that type of day, you feel like kicking a couple of holes in your wall!

When days go well, we are happy. When days go bad, we are sad. That is natural; however, I remember a day when I came in the door after school, threw my books down in the chair, yelled at my mom, stepped on my cat Rusty's tail, went into my room, slammed the door, threw myself down on my bed, and felt like crying. What was strange was that I had no reason to cry. It had not been a bad day. In fact, it had been a pretty good one. I decided that growing from child to adult just makes you do things like that sometimes. Thank God that our parents and our pets forgive us.

I've noticed something else that really shifts my mood. Have you every noticed that if ten people give you a compliment, and one person says something awful about you, you are more likely to remember the bad comment than the good ones? When this happens you get angry, and it is easy to stay angry. Then, you get angry with someone else, and they get angry at you, and you get more angry.

Some people like the roller coaster way of life. They get used to being angry, and think that it makes happier times even better. Others hate being angry or sad, and that makes them more angry and more sad.

I've found a better way to handle my highs and lows. When I'm feeling down and start to take it out on my family or friends, I ask God to forgive me. Then I work to bring His love into other peoples' lives. Smiling, giving another person a compliment, or doing a favor for another person can even out the highs and lows we experience.

Dear Jesus, help me to accept highs and lows, but in all times, help me to depend on Your love. And let Your love guide me to show more love to others. Amen.

But My Friends Do It

by Steven Schnarr

"You have this problem with responsibility, don't you? You just waltz right in here and . . . "

I have this real cool arrangement with my parents. Our house is divided into two complete halves. They live on one side, with me on the other; the only connection between the two sections is this neat little tube that regularly spews out twenty dollar bills. Of course we each have our own garages and cars . . .

"Are you listening to me, young man?" my father yelled at me, jarring my brain back to reality.

As I gently rubbed my eyes and tried to focus on his beet-red face, I was barely able to suppress a groan.

"Look at me when I talk to you! How can you expect me to trust you when you haven't the common courtesy to . . . "

You know the rest.

It happens to all of us. The art of parent-teen communication is a lot like riding a teeter-totter on the summit of Mount Everest —only your parents weigh a lot more than you do. One miscalculated maneuver on either party's side, and the whole apparatus goes crashing down the sheer slopes of the peak.

"Well, then, how do I communicate with my parents?" you might ask. "They don't let me do anything. All I do is ask, and all they do is refuse. It's like talking to a broken record! I wish I had freedom, like some of my friends!"

Of course, while you are reading this profound statement, your parents are complaining to their friends, "My kid just doesn't seem to want to listen to what I say. I'm trying to do what's best, but after a while I hear myself sounding like a broken record."

It seems like for all of the differences between you and your parents, you share a lot in common. Since both of you want to communicate with one another, the most important thing to do is to open the lines of communication. You can do this by trying not to hold a grudge and being as honest as possible. Once you start lying to your parents it becomes harder to stop, until one day there is no trust at all. Before they can trust you, you have got to give them some reason to trust you. Lastly, don't compare your family and your parents with other parents.

You need to realize that your teenage years will be a lot easier if you are friends with your parents, rather than holding them at arms' length. You might ask yourself, "What roadblocks can I remove that might cause my parents to say no?" One obstacle is a severed communication line between you and your parents, made of grudges, lies, and comparisons.

As your communication ties become stronger, it becomes easier to listen to each other and to compromise with each other. Your Heavenly Father loves you and is waiting to bless your family's communication.

To begin this sort of ideal relationship, especially if you are already off to a bad start, ask your parents to sit down and openly talk to you about it. Nothing can heal the festering wounds of a rough relationship like an honest, open conversation. Remember God is behind efforts to clear things up. He tells us that good family relationships are the basis for living a full life.

Dear God, please hold our teeter-totter steady, so my parents and I can work things out on level ground. Amen.

Loss

by Anne Hall

It was almost midnight, and I was still cutting and pasting photographs for my constitution notebook, which was due the next day. My fingers were trembling as I tried to work quickly. My nervousness made it almost impossible to accomplish anything. My stomach was tied in knots because tomorrow would be the first time I appeared as a cheerleader at our junior high wrestling match. Why was everything happening to me at once? Why was life suddenly so complicated and stressful? Sitting with my head in my hands I wished that I could go back to elementary school, where life, it seemed, had been so much easier.

Thoughts and feelings like these were very common when I was in junior high. I was involved in many extra activities, and I was expected to start acting grown up and being responsible. I often felt sad, because I thought that I had lost my old elementary school world, where life had been simpler. I knew that I could never go back to the way it was, and that was frightening. Gone were the days in which I did not have a care in the world, and so much less was expected of me. I even found myself thinking that I had lost control of my life.

Another kind of loss I experienced during this time in my life was the loss of my dad when he had to work out of state. My family and I lived in Alaska, but my dad worked in Missouri. He would work in Missouri for five weeks, and then he would come home for a one-week visit. This arrangement lasted for almost a year. I remember how much I missed him when he was gone, and how I could not really talk to him when he would call from his hotel room three thousand miles away.

When my father would finally get to come home for a visit, I always felt a little strange and awkward with him. His visits never seemed to last long enough that I could really relax with him. I often felt like I did not really have a dad. I would look at my friends and their dads, and feel like I was losing out because my dad was gone so much of the time.

Loss is something that everyone deals with during their life in some way or another. Loss can come in many ways, such as the loss of childhood innocence, or the loss of a loved one. Even though it hurts, it is always something that we must grow through. Although it may sometimes seem that you are all alone in your loss, or that you are losing everything, it is important to remember that God will always be with you to comfort you and see you to better days.

Dear Lord, please help me not to focus on the losses in my life, but instead give thanks for the blessings You give to me everyday. Amen.

Homosexuality

by Karen Zima

"Jennifer, I hate to be the one to tell you this, but I think your boyfriend Joe is gay."

Has anyone ever told you something like that? Or maybe someone told you that your best friend since third grade is a lesbian. Or that your own brother, the star basketball player, might be a "pretty boy." No matter what you hear, or how truthful it is, the suggestion of homosexuality is very awkward and difficult. Many people get utterly embarrassed when the subject comes up. Others may make jokes about it. Still others will simply avoid the subject altogether. But, no matter how much someone may not want to admit it, problems with homosexuality exist. Homosexuality has often been a well-kept secret in our society. Perhaps the worst thing about homosexuality is all the conflicting emotions that come along with it—both for those who are worried that they are gay, and for those whose friends and family members think that they are.

So now you might ask—with all the new changes in my life—how do I deal with the homosexuality issue too? Granted, it is not easy. But the same God who helps you every day of your life will help you deal with this problem too.

When my cousin's friend, Jennifer, heard that her boyfriend might be gay, she was devastated. First of all, she had no idea if it was true or not, and second, she was afraid to ask Joe (her boyfriend) about it. To make things even worse, all kinds of emotions seemed to bombard her at once. She felt hurt, confused, scared, and embarrassed. The rumor quickly got around school, and Jennifer feared that everybody was talking about her, and laughing at her behind her back. She was miserable.

Joe's best friend, Matt, felt as confused as Jennifer. Matt was afraid to even say "hi" to Joe anymore, for fear people would accuse him of being a homosexual too. But Matt knew that something had to be done. He could not just stand around and hope this would be over soon. Joe had been his best friend since they were babies; they told each other everything. And Joe must have heard the rumor by now. How did he feel? So Matt called Jennifer and Joe, and the three of them got together at Matt's house to talk about it.

At first, all three were really hesitant to talk. But soon, each one opened up. Joe admitted that he had, in fact, been having some confusing feelings lately. He had talked to the school counselor and his pastor about it—someone must have overheard. He felt just as emotionally overwhelmed as the other two; however, he told them that his faith had been helping him to deal with the situation. His pastor had told him that, although homosexual practice is a sin, a tendency towards homosexuality is not. And if Joe truly faced that problem, it was a temptation God would help him overcome. He also knew that through prayer, God would hear his questions and troubles, and would help him get through this time of searching. But what Joe stressed most was that he needed Jennifer and Matt's love and support. Without his close friends, he knew he could not handle this.

Jennifer, Joe, and Matt are still struggling with this issue. Each one continues to have many conflicting emotions. However, it has been much easier because of their love and understanding for one another, and because of their faith in God. Each day they pray and trust that God will help them work things out.

If you are struggling with the homosexuality issue, talk to someone you trust—a friend, parent, pastor, or counselor. And remember to talk to God. He is there to help you.

Dear God, please be with me during these troubling times. When I worry about my sexuality or the feelings of a friend, help me to know that You understand my hurt, my confused feelings, and my fear. Help me to remember that You will always love and forgive me, and that You will always be here for me, no matter what. In Jesus' name. Amen.

I'm the Youngest

by Joy Mason

I felt like screaming. Either that, or punching old Aunt Tilda in the nose. If I heard another word about how great my older sister Cathy was, I think I honestly would do one or the other.

"I just have to say, your sister is so smart," Aunt Tilda went on, unaware of my mood. "And so talented! I heard she did a great job of taking care of you and your father when your mother was away. You are so lucky to have a sister like that."

Yeah, right, I thought, smiling politely. Oh, yes. It was so wonderful to have a sister like Cathy. She was great at everything she did, whether it was cooking or writing or music, or even just talking to people. And no one seemed able to stop talking about all her great accomplishments. It was so frustrating. I always got A's in English, and could play just as many instruments as she, but did anyone ever notice? I was beginning to think not.

I threaded my way through the relatives that had come to our house for a family reunion, trying to avoid talking to anyone. I started to turn away when I saw Cathy talking to an uncle, but she caught my eye and motioned me over.

"I was just telling Uncle Roger about your basketball game last Friday," Cathy said, and for some reason, I could almost sense a bit of pride in her voice.

"Yeah, I read someplace that you had been ranked fifth in state," Uncle Roger said, giving me a one-armed hug.

I was having trouble believing he was actually interested in talking about something having to do with me. I kind of half-smiled. "Actually, it's fourth place."

"Fourth! Wow, that's impressive. Hey, keep it up—that ability could be worth a good scholarship some day." Uncle Roger hugged me again and turned to talk to someone else.

As soon as his back was turned, Cathy rolled her eyes. "You know, that's all I've been hearing all day—great things about my little sister, the great basketball star."

I must have looked at her strangely, because she laughed. "Yeah. All these people keep coming up to me and asking me how my sister is and how her team is doing. I keep telling them they should ask you."

"But everyone I talk to goes on and on about *you*. About how great you are at this, and how great you are at that. I feel like I'm related to the president."

Cathy laughed. "Maybe it's time these relatives got us sisters straight. You're good at what you're good at, and I'm good at what I'm good at. It'd sure be nice if I could hear what they think of me!"

I laughed, feeling much better about the whole thing. "So," I asked Cathy, "what were they saying about me, anyway?"

Dear Lord, help me to recognize and be thankful for the talents that You have given me, and not be jealous of my siblings' gifts. Amen.

I'm the Oldest

by Joanna Rosenberg

"Stop changing the channels. I had the TV on first!" Bobby yelled.

As Samantha's brother ran up to the TV to push the button for Channel 12, she whipped out the remote and changed it back to Channel 31. "Bobby, just leave it on this channel."

"No! I was here first!"

"Bobby, you know we both agreed that you get the TV from 4:00 to 6:00, and I get it from 6:00 to 8:00. Guess what time it is. It's 6:00, and it's my turn to watch TV."

"MOM!" yelled Bobby.

As Mom came down the stairs, Bobby and Samantha were still fighting, only this time Samantha was sitting on top of him, so he wouldn't get up and change the channel again.

"What is all this yelling about?"

"Mom," Bobby complained from where he was, squished under Samantha, "Samantha won't let me watch my cartoon, and I want to watch it."

"But, Mom, Bobby and I agreed that he gets the TV for two hours, and then I get it. His two hours are up!"

"Samantha, can I talk to you?" Mom asked.

Well, during the next 20 minutes or so that seemed like an eternity to Samantha, Mom explained that since Samantha was the oldest she should set a good example, and so on. So Bobby got to watch TV, while Samantha sat in her room for yelling at her mom.

When Samantha told me about it, I remembered a lot of similar experiences with my own brother. I used to dream up schemes to get even with him, and wonder why I always got the blame. Maybe you get into fights with your brothers and sisters,

79

and end up not speaking to each other for two or three days. But here's something that makes me smile; maybe it will make you smile too:

- You are most likely a role model to your younger brother or sister.
- They look up to you in many ways.
- They ask you for help with their problems.
- You'll end up being better pals after all the hard times.
- You get your driver's license first, which means you'll get out of the house more often.
- You don't end up getting all the old worn clothes from older brothers and sisters.

Last, but not least:

- You'll always love each other.

Dear God, please help me be patient with my younger sibling. Strengthen our relationship, and forgive us when we don't get along. Amen.

"Your time is up in exactly 17 seconds."

When My Grandma Died

by Rachel Goetzke and Gretchen Ricker

At first I thought I was in trouble when my mother motioned for me to come to her. "What did I do?" I asked.

"You didn't do anything," she replied. "Grandma had a stroke."

We were on a trip at the time, so we flew to the hospital as soon as we could. I did not know if Grandma would be alive when we got there. My grandma had not been sick before, and I did not understand how she could be in the hospital in a coma so suddenly.

A friend of mine told me that God just wanted Grandma with Him more than He wanted her with me. That made me really mad.

"Well, God can't have her," I snapped.

Grandma was taken to the hospital on Friday. I was there almost every day. She died on Tuesday.

I felt sad, but my feelings of sorrow were more for my dad and Grandpa than for my loss of Grandma. It wasn't that I did not care; I felt that their grief was more important than mine. I tried to be the perfect daughter, so I wouldn't cause my dad any more stress.

After my grandma died, I did not know whether to sit at home with my family, go to my room, cry all the time, try to cheer people up, or do things with my friends. I put my grief on hold for a while; I thought only of what my family needed. This was not a very wise thing to do. It all came out later, and, when it did, no one else could understand what was happening. For instance, I went out with one of my friends, and when I came home I broke down and cried on his shoulder. This is the way I finally let it out, but now I think it would have been easier if I let it out when everyone else did. A friend of mine could not look at her grandmother's body at the funeral. It was not that she was denying the death. She just could not handle the emotional strain of seeing her grandmother dead at that time with all those people around.

When someone dies, you will go through stages of grief. You will need to handle your grief in your own way—crying, holding back tears, talking with your family.

One feeling you may have at this time is anger. You might be angry at God for the death of the person you loved, or you might even be angry at yourself—you might wish you had said or done something differently before the person died. Tell God about your anger. He will understand. He let His own Son die and rise again to conquer death. He will lead you through your grief.

God, help me to get over the loss of the person I loved, and thank You for the time we got to spend together. In Jesus' name. Amen.

It's Okay to Cry!

by Daniel Gunderman and Karen Zima

Have you ever been sitting in a movie theater, when all of a sudden the person next to you starts sniffling and sobbing so loud that you can hardly hear the movie? Most likely that person was Karen. She is an extremely emotional person. She cries at movies, funerals, graduations, good-byes, and even when she laughs. She even gets incredibly emotional over half-hour sitcoms! However, I will tell you this: She is not a wimp, and neither are you, if you cry. Crying is a natural part of being human. It is not any more feminine than masculine. It is not a sign of weakness. Some people may just be more sensitive than others, or maybe it is easier for them to cry than to hold in emotion.

Many guys seem to have a hard time crying. I am an eighteen-year-old male heading off to college next year, and I have a good cry at least once a month. It is a time when I let it all come out: A full month of built-up emotion in the form of frustration and anxiety. Usually something unimportant and seemingly stupid sets it off. I remember once I was learning a Shakespearean monologue for a final in an acting class, and I could not do it. That was the spark. I cried for an hour after that. Afterwards I felt better. No! I felt great!

For some reason, society has put a rule on guys, making it uncool to cry. Well, I hate to break it to you, but many girls have told me that they like a sensitive guy. A close, female friend of mine told me, "A guy who cries is not afraid of what people may think of him. I can really admire that!"

Sometimes I think girls have it easier when it comes to expressing emotions. Of course, I could be wrong, but society accepts female crying. However, girls, do not be fooled into thinking that you are just "weak little women." That is not true either. In our society, women are seen as more outwardly sensitive than men, yet they are equally as strong, or stronger than men, in handling stressful situations.

Whether you are a boy or girl, how do you deal with the teasing? There are some people who just will not let you cry without hassling you about it. Try to remember that you are not a wimp, just because you shed a few tears. Crying is a part of life. Most likely, those that tease about crying may need a good cry themselves. Ask the Lord to help you accept the fact that you are human, and ask Him to help you realize that if you do cry, it does not make you any weaker than the next person.

Dear God, sometimes my tears mean I need You. Help me to release my fears and joys to You in my tears and prayers. Amen.

"That's beautiful, simply beautiful."

I Don't Want Them to Be My Friends

by Amy B. Frerichs

I was walking home from school when I heard someone yell, "Hey, Amy! Wait for me!"

Oh great, I thought, it was Julie, the last person I wanted to be seen walking home with. I had known her for a couple of years, and I considered her an acquaintance, but Julie thought that we were the best of friends. It seemed like she was always hanging around me at school, and she constantly phoned my house at night. I had my own group of friends, and Julie really didn't fit in with them. Everyone at school thought that she was a nerd, so I was embarrassed to even be seen with her. After all, I was part of the popular group, and to be seen with a nerd was just unheard of.

Julie was a nice person, and I could tell that she really wanted to be accepted, but what would my friends think if I was nice to her? I tried to be nice to her when my friends were not around, but the rest of the time I ignored her. I really began to feel bad, but I could not tell her why I would not talk to her around my friends. The easiest thing to do would be to ignore her, so I thought.

That day as we walked home, Julie burst into tears. She told me that she was upset because I had been ignoring her lately. She thought that we were friends, and she was really hurt.

"So why have you been ignoring me?" Julie asked.

I was so stunned, I had no idea what to say. What could I say? At first, I thought that I should go ahead and tell her that she was a nerd, but that just was not the right thing to do. It would have been mean. After all, who was I to call her a nerd?

What would God have wanted me to do? That is a question that many of us forget to ask.

In Romans 15:7, it says, "Accept one another, then, just as Christ accepted you, in order to bring praise to God." Accept one another! That was not what I was doing! God wants us to accept other people, the way they are. Many times we accept only those whom we like, or those who dress and act like us, or those whom we want to like us. God accepts each of us just the way we are, through the saving work of Jesus. God's example can help us accept others.

I was in a difficult situation that I had created for myself. If you had been in the same situation, what would you have done? Would you have had the courage to take a stand and accept Julie as your friend, always, not just when your friends were not around? Or would you have gone on pretending? I know that this is a hard question, and even harder when it actually happens to you. It takes a lot of courage to accept others who do not fit in.

Sometimes we are cruel to people, and God forgives us and gives us strength to try again. A helpful question I have found to ask myself in tough situations is, "If God were standing beside me, what would I do?" God is always standing beside us, and maybe He's saying, "Love this person just like I love you!"

Lord, please guide me as I face the challenges of life. Forgive me when I get so caught up in friends and popularity that I forget those who are not in my group. Help me to remember that You always accept me and walk beside me. Amen.

You Can Be a Truck Driver!

by Jennifer Ashby

"Hey you guys! We need a few strong boys to help unload this truck!" shouted Mr. Adams.

Today was the annual youth paper drive at the church. All the funds would go to the summer youth trip. When Mr. Adams called for some people to help, several boys headed for the truck. Not knowing what to expect, Maggy joined them.

"Okay, let's get to work, guys!" directed Mr. Adams, the youth minister.

"Check out Maggy," screamed Mark. "She's moving more than you, Josh. What's wrong, too weak?"

"Okay," said Mr. Adams, "lay off, guys. You know that women can do things as well or better than men. Just because Maggy is female doesn't mean that she can't do something."

Mr. Adams reminded the group of the incident at Bible study the next day. "There are many examples of women doing God's work in the Bible," he said. "Take the woman at the well, for instance. Jesus walked up to her, and she didn't even know who He was or what He could do. She believed His every word, then went back to her town and brought the people to see Jesus!"

"So what, that's one woman in the entire Bible that did something good," cracked Josh.

"Have you ever heard of Deborah, or Mary Magdalene?" questioned Maggy.

"What? More women?" Mark asked, pretending to be shocked.

"Yes, as a matter of fact, Mary Magdalene was the first person to see Jesus after He had risen from the dead, and she told the disciples Jesus was alive," stated Maggy.

"And who is Deborah?" asked Mark.

Mr. Adams jumped in. "I'll answer that one, Maggy. Deborah was a female judge who led the children of Israel in defeating some of their enemies who worshiped false gods."

"So all right already, we get your point. Girls are able to do things too," admitted Mark.

"You know there is a verse found in Galatians, chapter 3, that says, 'There is neither Jew nor Greek, slave nor free, male nor female, for you are all one in Christ Jesus.' This tells us that we are all equal in the Lord's sight."

"So what's your point, Mr. A?" Mark asked.

"My point is, boys, just remember that the girls can be truck drivers too."

Lord, let us all look at each other as equals in Your sight. Help us to use our talents, and recognize talents in others too. Amen.

"Anyone want to join me for a yogurt?"

What If I Die?

by Susan Van Dermeulen

Lying in bed in the silent darkness, thoughts rushed through my head. What would I be like when I grew up? Would I get married? What would the world be like then? One thought, no matter how hard I tried to make it go away, would not leave. What would happen if I died? Although it may sound stupid, the question really bothered me. Would I be prepared to die if I was in a car accident? Would I go to heaven?

After I thought about those questions, my head started swimming with more and more—things like the world ending, and people getting killed by the spread of AIDS. I was so confused. Although this was something I had no control over, I had to figure out what I thought about the subject. So, I looked up "death" in the Bible, and one verse in particular popped out.

In Psalm 23:4 I found, "Even though I walk through the valley of the shadow of death, I will fear no evil, for You are with me; Your rod and Your staff, they comfort me."

So what do I believe? Am I prepared to die? Will I go to heaven? Death scares me. I am afraid of my parents dying, of my grandparents dying, of anyone dying. How can I face my own death? "Even though I walk through the valley of the shadow of death . . . You are with me."

King David wrote those words and King David had the answer. He knew no matter how close he, or a friend, was to death, God was with him. God was there to comfort him.

God does not tell us exactly what death is like. He does not tell us when and where our death may come. But God does take away the fear of death with the promise that He will be with us forever. He has given us the assurance of a heavenly home with Him through the death and resurrection of His only Son, Jesus Christ.

Death still frightens me. Oh, I am not afraid that I am not prepared, because I know that God will prepare me. Nor am I scared that I will not go to heaven. I know I will be in heaven because of Jesus Christ. But not knowing when or how I will die still scares me a little. It helps to know that the Lord will be there with me if I get frightened; and, if I have questions about anything, He provides parents, ministers, teachers, and friends to help me to understand.

Lord, please grant me the strength to accept the fact of death and to thank You for being there with me, so I do not have to be alone. Amen.

What Can I Do to Help?

by Cari A. Kuppler

The two gunshots were so loud they made the buildings shake. Not thinking of her own safety, a woman ran down the alley. She saw a boy lying by a dumpster like a piece of discarded trash. She began calling for help, but no one responded.

Looking down at herself, she understood why her cries were ignored. She was dressed in tattered and dirty clothing. She was homeless. She wasn't important.

The woman was thinking about giving up when two young boys came running to her. She explained what had happened, and the two boys ran off to phone for assistance. When help arrived, the boys asked the homeless woman if there was anything they could do for her. She thanked them for responding to her cry for help, and told them they had done more than enough already.

"You are two very special people," commented the woman. "How old are you?"

"I'm twelve, and my friend is thirteen," replied the younger boy.

"Not many people your age would have taken the time to help someone like me," said the woman, looking down at herself.

"What do you mean, someone like you?" asked one of the boys.

The woman replied in surprise, "I find my clothes in trash dumpsters. I am homeless, and people usually ignore me."

"We didn't even think about your being homeless," the boys explained. "You needed help, and when someone calls for help, they should not be ignored."

A few days later, the woman walked into a shelter where she sometimes came for a hot meal and a shower. To her sur-

94

prise, the two young boys from the alley came running up to her. They sat and talked for a while, and the boys explained that they volunteered to help serve meals at the shelter one day a week. The homeless woman enjoyed their visit more than the meal they served her.

Stories like this one happen every day. There are many people in our world who need help. Some are oceans away, but there are many who are very close to us, even next door. You can make a difference in the lives of some needy people, and no one is too young to help someone who needs it. Ask a parent, teacher, youth director, or pastor for some ways that you can help.

If something like serving meals at a shelter seems scary, try to find some other ways to help. Consider helping with a food and clothing drive for the needy, or cleaning up a neighborhood playground or parkway, or sponsoring a child. You can make a difference! And you can always help others simply by praying for them. The Lord does not care how old or rich you are. He listens to everyone!

Dear Lord, please give me the strength, the courage, and, if necessary, the loud voice I need to encourage others to help those who need it. In the name of Christ. Amen.

I'm Too . . .

by Cyndi Pahl

Kathy walked home slowly from the bus stop. In her mind she could hear the voices of her classmates yelling, "Bye, bean-pole!" "Don't hit the ceiling!" "What a toothpick!" "Is she from Ethiopia?"

Why are people so mean? Kathy wondered. I can't help how I am, can I? So, I am tall and skinny, so what! But maybe, if I slouched a little, yeah, like that. I feel shorter. Hmmm, if I walk like this maybe I'll look shorter, and then they won't tease me so much.

You and I know that Kathy might feel better for a little bit while she slouches, but that really is not the best solution.

How about Keith? His problem was different, but just as frustrating.

Keith could feel his face turning red. It always did every time he saw *her*. Her name was Monika and she was the loveliest creature on earth. But he had never talked to her. He wanted to, but the thought of approaching her choked him up, and he could not speak.

What if I say something stupid, and she laughs at me, he thought. He shuddered, remembering how he had made a fool of himself yesterday.

He had passed her in the hall, and she had looked at him and smiled, and said, "Hi, Keith."

Monika had spoken to him! He was so flustered he did not even smile back, let alone say hi! He just stared at her, and ran into the people walking in front of him, dropping his books everywhere. He could have died! It was so embarrassing. Now she probably thought he was a nerd. Why couldn't he talk to her like a normal guy? Why was he so shy?

Kathy and Keith are not alone, right? Other kids have frustrating feelings too. Although it is not fun, it is a part of growing up. Have you ever found yourself thinking one of these thoughts?

I do not feel like a part of the group.
My clothes are really out of style.
I am stupid.
Why can't I be more like them?
No one likes me!
I do not feel like I belong.
I hate the way I look.
I am out of it.
I will never be popular.

At times, we all feel left out and alone, not sure of ourselves. We compare ourselves to the people we like, or those we want to be like, and we usually fall short. You might think that everyone is better than you are, and that they have something you do not. These are thoughts common to all of us. If they bother you all the time, try talking to someone—a close friend or relative, a pastor or youth minister, a teacher or counselor. People who care about you will remind you—God loves you as you are. He will help you learn to accept yourself.

Dear Lord, help me to remember that it is what is on the inside of me that really counts. Help me to learn to accept myself and others for who we are, and help me to remember that You accept me and love me, no matter what. Amen.

" I don't seem to be making
a good impression."

You're Not a Loser— Relationships with Teachers

by Elizabeth Strubbe

I will always remember Alex. It seemed our teacher was constantly picking on him. We were only in kindergarten, but it was still obvious. Whenever he was reading and couldn't quite sound out a word, our teacher would slap the back of his head or pull his ear, as if that would help him speak or gain his concentration. Like most kids who are treated unfairly, Alex would laugh the incident off, but I could tell he was really embarrassed by it.

Alex wasn't a loser—the teacher just treated him like one. She would even put his desk at the very front of the classroom so he was always right in her reach. I always felt sorry for Alex, especially since he was a good friend of mine.

Why do teachers treat some students so insensitively? There is probably not one good answer to that question, but it is a situation that, many times, can be turned around.

Instead of sulking or taking actions of retaliation against your teacher, show him or her what your Christianity makes you. Keep in mind that the teacher is not always the main problem. Start with yourself. If you respect a teacher, he or she will most likely respect you back. It is a basic response of human nature.

If you are still having problems, take Jesus' example from Matthew 18. Talk to the teacher one-on-one if you continue to feel that you are being treated unfairly. Teachers should also be made aware of problems at home, or of other things on your mind, so they can understand a change of attitude on your part. Most teachers try to be understanding. If you bring an unfairness to their attention, they will work to improve that part of their life and make it easier for you.

Since you share the same space with your teacher almost every day of the week, try to be on good terms with him or her. Good teachers are out there and like to deal on a more personal level with their students outside of the classroom.

Above all else, if you are still feeling put down, remember Jesus. He was picked on and persecuted by the teachers of His day—the Pharisees. And yet He continued with the work His Father had sent Him to do, and He forgave those who treated Him unfairly. Jesus will always build you up and love you for exactly what you are.

Dear Jesus, bless my dealings with my teachers, and help me to love them as You love me. Amen.

Why I Like Boys

by Erica Christian

Look at that guy. Isn't he cute? Oh, no! He's coming over here! I can't smile because half of my lunch is caught in my braces. Does anybody have a toothpick?

Men! Who needs 'em? Have you heard that before? Yet when you see a cute guy, all these self-conscious thoughts race through your head.

What am I going to say? What am I going to do?

Does he think my thighs are huge?

I haven't brushed my hair since noon!

Does any of this sound familiar to you? Have you ever found yourself feeling self-conscious around a cute guy? The fact is, though, that even though they cause confusing feelings, I need men. But what do I do, and *how* do I need them?

Should guys simply be my friends—or do I want more than that? I think that is a question often asked by girls our age. Are you confused about guys and where you stand?

Most of the guys I hang around with are friends. It's not because I am so ugly they would never want to date me. I find it more fun to have guys as friends instead of boyfriends, because I can just be myself and I don't have to constantly worry about my appearance. I'm not saying it's wrong to date guys. In fact, I like to date! I just have more guys that are friends than guys that I date.

Now, if you don't have any of these feelings, that is okay! People develop physically and emotionally at different rates, and it doesn't matter if you do not want to date or be around guys just now. I assure you, though, that your day will come. And believe me—you will want to date. We are all different people, going through different stages at different times. So trust me—your time will come!

You know, God created women and God created men. His intention was and is for us to be together.

So let the good times roll! Have fun with the guys, and remember to be yourself. God is with you—even in puberty.

Dear Lord, please be with me and help me to make the right choices in my relationships, both now and in the future. Amen.

*" That guy is darling! My lunch is hanging
out of my braces! Quick, who has a toothpick?"*

Why I Like Girls

by Ryan Smith

I was walking down the hallway when I accidentally brushed against Stephanie. Now, there was nothing special about Stephanie. She was just a girl in my pre-algebra class, but for some unexplained reason, I felt warm inside. It was almost as if I enjoyed this contact with a girl. I thought that this could not be true, though, because just a few months ago I would have been pulling her hair, or launching spit wads at her from the back row of the classroom.

The school year was rolling along and the Winter Mixer was coming up. The next thing I knew, I was asking Stephanie to go to the dance with me. Even more strange was the fact that many of the other guys who had been my accomplices in the spit wad crimes began to talk and interact with girls.

As I look back on these experiences, I realize that that time was a turning point in my life. I was now happy to have friends that were girls. I could study with girls, and talk to girls, and still be considered normal.

Maybe you're experiencing feelings like mine right now. Or maybe it will be a while yet before you get interested in taking a girl out. Don't worry about it. Do what's right for you. I realized the Lord has blessed me by giving me relationships with both boys and girls. He will do the same for you.

Jesus, please help me to like and respect girls and to be friends with them. Amen.

What Do I Do When I Don't Like How I Look?

by Kiphany Elmshauser

"I hate this skirt! It makes me look disgustingly gross," said Gwen as she stood in front of the mirror. Gwen knew that her problem was not the skirt, but rather her body. She hated her body; she was a giant living in a world of midgets. How come all of the other girls in seventh grade were shaped liked sticks, but she had to have curves, bulges, and bumps? She wondered if God really wanted her to be the "oddball." Gwen was frightened and lonely, trapped in a body she did not want. She was fat, and that was all there was to say.

Amazingly enough, almost all girls and boys go through a certain stage when they are just not satisfied with their bodies. For some kids, it is only a phase, but for others, the frustration lasts throughout their lifetime. How do you cope with a body you are stuck with, but do not particularly like?

The first thing to remember is that *you are not alone!* Even though you feel like the goofiest looking one at your school, chances are your closest friends are feeling the same way. Appearance has become very important in society today. The size you happen to be becomes especially important when you start noticing and comparing yourself to everyone else.

What can you do when you do not like your appearance? It's good to remember that God gave us the gift to have love and compassion for others *and* for ourselves. It is impossible to love someone else when you do not truly love yourself.

God gave you your body. Respecting and accepting your body is the first step in loving yourself. God created you to be beautiful. Remember this saying, "God don't make no trash"?

It is true—no matter what size, shape, or color we are, we are *all* beautiful in God's eyes. Coming to grips with the physical body God has given us will make us a lot happier. After all, He loves us no matter what!

Dear God, please help me to love what You have given me. Remind me that I was created to praise You. Amen.

Next Week? Next Year? What about Today?

by Brian Fiedler

Everyone pesters me about what I want to do with my life. "Where are you going to high school?" "What college do you want to attend?" "What do you want to be when you grow up?"

I really wish people would quit bugging me. Who cares about the future; I am worried about today! I have so many things to worry about now, I don't even want to think about the future! With school, sports, friends, and my family, I have no time to consider what I will do when I grow up.

We all get frustrated at times by the demands placed on us. Adults expect so much from us, like good grades. We want to get good grades, too, and be the star basketball player, have a lot of friends—not to mention a special boyfriend or girlfriend. And parents want us to be good Christian children on top of all of this. After a while, it seems like you get pulled under by all of the demands.

In the Bible, God says that He will be our strength and our shield. I think that this means, when we feel down about all of the demands and we can not see a way out of them, all we need to do is to pray, asking God for help. His help may not come in an immediate miracle, but He does answer prayer, and things will get better.

I will not say that your life will be easy, or that everything you try will turn out perfectly, but if you are watching, you will see a difference if you ask God for help. You may notice that schoolwork will be less of a hassle, you may come out of a slump in sports, or you may settle a disagreement with a friend. Maybe you will just get better at getting along with the pressures.

The Bible also says that God will be a shield for you. Whenever you are tempted to do something that you know is wrong, God will lead you. He will help you to resist temptation and make a better decision. The temptation may always be there, but it will not be as strong or as difficult to resist if you have God's help.

As for the future, it is good to think about it, pray about it, and talk to parents and counselors about it, so you can do some preparing for what is ahead. It is not good to worry about it. God will be with you in your future too. Remember, our lives belong to Him, and He will guide us and protect us forever. He might lead you to become a pastor or teacher, or maybe into a profession that is not church-related, where you can still serve Him. God will lead you to witness in any job you do. There are so many possibilities, but in everything, let God be your strength and shield. He will help you handle your demands today and in the future.

Almighty God, help me through hard times. Remind me that You are always with me. Help me to keep You as the main focus in life and not become too worried about my future. Amen.

My Friends Have More Money

by Jason Kaspar

I remember it so clearly, it seems like it just happened yesterday.

The eighth grade class at my school took a trip to Chicago every spring. I looked forward to the trip my whole eighth grade year. We worked on a lot of projects to earn money for transportation and housing.

A few days before the trip, I asked my parents for some spending money. Dad said finances were tight and that he couldn't give me much. I said that was fine, still expecting maybe fifty or sixty dollars. My friend, Tom, told me that his parents had given him sixty dollars without even thinking about it.

When Dad handed me thirty dollars, I was surprised. It didn't seem like much, but I thought I could handle it.

When I got to school Friday morning, some of the kids were flashing around seventy and eighty dollars! I didn't say a word. I felt bad, but how many souvenirs could you buy in Chicago?

Well, I found out. I tried to be careful with my money. But every time a bunch of guys bought a t-shirt or an extra hot dog, I felt like I had to join in. I never realized money could go so fast.

By the time we got to the Cubs game Saturday night, my money was gone. I tried not to notice Tom next to me as he downed peanuts and soda and ice cream. Around the seventh inning, Tom asked me if I wasn't getting hungry.

Hungry? I was starved. It was pretty embarrassing, but I told Tom I had run out of money. He was a generous and understanding friend. He loaned me $2.00 right away for something to eat. And the next day at the Museum of Science and Industry, Tom just walked up and gave me some money for lunch. I told him I would pay him back as soon as we got home, but Tom said to forget it.

Looking back on that trip, it seems kind of funny that buying souvenirs and junk food was such a big deal. But it is hard to be the one in the crowd that does not have enough money. And I know a lot of kids have it a lot worse than I did.

God saw me through that class trip with the help of a generous friend. I know I can trust Him to see me through all kinds of problems, and so can you. God paid a huge price—the death of His Son—to prove His love for us. And that kind of priceless love means a lot more than dollars and cents.

Lord, help me to realize that money is not the most important thing in my life. Help me to rely more on You. Amen.

Witness, or Not?

by Sarah Kaufmann

I was driving down the highway late one night with one of my friends. Suddenly I lost control of the car, and we swerved off the road and onto the shoulder. We weren't hurt, but I was so confused and afraid that I just sat there shaking.

A tractor-trailer pulled over onto the shoulder, and the driver got out to help me. I started talking about what had happened, and he must have seen the fear and confusion in my eyes because he said, "You should thank God you're alive, young lady."

It was then that I realized that I was not lucky or a good driver at all. God had protected me and my friend and everyone around. No one was injured. The truck driver told me where I could make a phone call. His advice was helpful, and I realize now that God had sent him to help me.

I used to wonder how I could go about showing my faith in my life. I really didn't feel like I could be a missionary and preach in a different country, or save dying children stricken by poverty. But when I tell my friends about that accident, I know I am witnessing my faith.

Witnessing is not necessarily going door to door with pamphlets and a speech. God grants us opportunities to witness when we least expect them. He doesn't expect everyone to "sing like angels" or "preach like Paul." It matters only how we use the gifts and the opportunities He gives us to live our faith.

Dear God, thank You for being with me in every moment of my life. Let my life be a witness to You. Amen.

111

Why Doesn't Dad Like My Music?

by Brian DeLunas

Loud rock and roll, hard-pumpin' rap, exciting dance music. For teens, music is a way of life. Everyone has a favorite type of music—that special music you turn on when you're feeling down. Or, the music that gets you excited and ready to dance.

Being a teenager, I know these feelings and like a variety of music, from hard rock to hard rap. I especially like the hard beats and low bass of my favorite rap groups. The sound of the music is great to my ears, but, unfortunately, not to my dad's.

I remember one night when I heard my favorite song coming on and rushed over to turn up the radio, only to be disappointed by my father's words, "Turn that junk off!" My father is a strong, Christian man who believes in sharing his faith with me. He sent me to a Christian grade school and high school when I could have just as well gone to a public school and saved him money.

Dad heard what I was listening to and disapproved. He didn't like the lyrics or the rap's message, and he told me he didn't want me listening to it.

Eventually, I did stop listening to that song, but it wasn't all because of my father's doings. I had to sit down and ask myself, Is this what Jesus wants me listening to? It didn't take me very long to figure out that Jesus didn't approve of me listening to a bunch of people cuss and say things that went against His teachings. Some groups even go so far as to suggest that Jesus is not God. That's where I had to draw the line. I mean, I was either for God or against Him. There is no in-between.

I'm not telling you to stop listening to your favorite songs. Just stop and listen to what the words are saying. Then ask yourself, Is this what God would want me to listen to?

God loves you, and He gave you music to enjoy. He says, "Shout for joy to the Lord, all the earth, burst into jubilant song with music" (Ps. 98:4).

Dear Heavenly Father, watch over the musical taste I have as a Christian, and let me make music to You always. Amen.

"Whatever happened to Bee Bumble and the Stingers?"

Driving Drunk

by Michael House

"Can you hear me, Michael?"

I could hear the voice echoing in my head over and over again. I felt numb all over. My head was wrapped with a white bandage and throbbing. I opened and closed my eyes, trying to see if what I saw was real. My left leg hung from metal chains in a big white cast showing only my toes. I looked around and saw my mother, father, and a doctor at the end of my bed.

The doctor looked at me and began to flip through his charts. He said, "You are very lucky. You were a tough one to stabilize. It's a good thing you are so healthy, or you probably wouldn't have made it."

My mother asked me how I felt. I mumbled, "It hurts a little." The doctor gave me a quick physical and left the room.

My father asked me if I knew what had happened. I thought for a moment. Then it hit me all at once. Dad asked me if I wanted to talk about it, but I said, "Not now."

Later, as I was lying in bed in the dark hospital room, I could no longer avoid thinking about what had happened. I decided to think through the whole situation.

My friends and I had it all planned out: It was going to be a great Friday night. We were on our way to a party—not a big deal, just a few friends getting together.

When my friends and I got to the party, it was unbelievable. There must have been 50 cars outside! No one said anything. We just looked at each other and ran inside.

There were people everywhere, but hardly anyone I knew. Everything was quiet until an older guy came through the door and yelled, "Party Time!" A few more guys ran outside and came right back with cases of beer.

I felt a little worried, but as the night progressed, I had a wonderful time.

Even though I didn't drink, I had a lot of fun. I met a lot of people and danced with some nice girls. I even got a few phone numbers.

As it got later, people started to leave. I decided I'd better gather up my friends—Dave, Carl, Brad, Tom, and Darren. I couldn't find Darren, but it turned out that he had found a gal, and she took him home. The others were bombed off their feet, and I became the designated driver.

As the five of us climbed into Brad's car, I made them all put their seat belts on. I dropped Dave and Carl off and still had Brad and Tom, the two wildest of the bunch.

As I was driving along Highway 21, Tom started to get sick. I pulled over, and we all got out. As I started back to the car, I found that Brad had run back to the car and was starting to drive away. I ran and hopped in the passenger seat and told him to stop. But Brad kept going.

He made it into traffic, but we were weaving all over the road. I knew I couldn't pull the keys out of the ignition because the wheel would lock up. I thought about shifting into park, but that would strip the gears, and Brad's mom would find out that he'd been drinking.

The last thing I remember was that we were going very fast, and we weren't on the road anymore.

I've heard these words a hundred times: Don't drink and drive. Friends don't let friends drive drunk. If you are not responsible, you will pay for it.

Those aren't just words anymore. Thanks to God's care, Brad and I are still alive. Don't think it can't happen to you. It can happen to anyone.

Dear Lord, help me make responsible decisions. Amen.

Accepting Yourself

by Indra Kradle

Wow, am I ugly, I sadly said to myself as I stared at my 7th grade school picture. The face in the picture surprised me. Huge, shiny braces that looked like railroad tracks lit up the photo. My electric blue eye shadow was messy under my slightly untamed eyebrows, making my brown eyes look uneven on my face. The huge, curly bangs—which were very fashionable— caused my cheeks to look round and chipmunk-like.

I sighed as I walked down the hall at school thinking about my situation. I was ugly, played in the nerdy school band, and I stayed home with my family on weekends. I was a geek and I knew it.

If only I could be like everyone else, I sighed to myself. I wished I could have the same clothes, hair, and face as all the rest of the girls who aren't geeks like me.

Then, that Christmas, I received a wonderful gift from my grandmother. It was a wooden plaque with a poem inscribed on it. I read it, amazed:

My Teen Years
It's not enough to have a dream,
Unless I'm willing to pursue it.
It's not enough to know what's right,
Unless I'm strong enough to do it.
It's not enough to join the crowd,
To be acknowledged and accepted—
I must be true to my ideals,
Even if I'm excluded and rejected.
It's not enough to learn the truth,
Unless I also learn to live it.

117

It's not enough to reach for love,
Unless I care enough to give it.
—Anonymous

From that point, I realized that there must have been millions of kids who felt rejected like me. It wasn't bad to be an individual. We are all unique people—specially created by God. After that Christmas break, I went back to school with a new attitude, a new self-image, and a glowing smile. I had never felt so self-confident in my life.

I am the only *me* in the entire world, so why not be different?

Dear God, thank You for creating me as an individual and for loving me just the way I am. Amen.

"I'd like to exchange my face, please."

Christmas and Cocaine

by Nikki Parmley

I loved going over to Granite City on Christmas Day. The whole family would go to my grandma and grandpa's house for a big Christmas dinner. One of those Christmases really stands out, because Aunt Sandy and Uncle Rob always acted so weird at Christmas time. They would never give gifts to anyone in the family. And they never let anyone give gifts to their son Tommy.

On that special Christmas—the Christmas of 1983—we were surprised to see Aunt Sandy and Uncle Rob bearing gifts for all the cousins. I will always remember the Barbie walkman my aunt picked out for me. I cried when I received it because I'd never received a gift from them in my life.

One week after that Christmas, Dad came home from work and took Mom into the bedroom, where they talked in whispers. I was hoping for late Christmas gifts they might have forgotten to give me, so I huddled by the door listening. Dad told Mom that Aunt Sandy was in a coma from a cocaine overdose. Tommy had found her in the living room, out cold, and dialed 911.

Two days later my aunt died. I don't remember if my parents went to the funeral. What I do remember is how angry my family was at Uncle Rob for letting his son be exposed to a drug-addicted mother.

One week after the funeral a warrant was made out for my uncle's arrest. He was going to be charged with manslaughter for giving my aunt cocaine. Uncle Rob got scared and ran from the law. For a while we would hear his name on TV and radio and see it in the newspaper. Then everything stopped. My parents never spoke about him.

The summer after my aunt died, Mom finally told me what had happened. Uncle Rob had not been convicted of manslaughter. But he was required to get help with his drug problem. Today Uncle Rob has married again and still lives in Granite City. He hasn't done drugs since Aunt Sandy died. Tommy still lives with his dad. I think the whole incident brought them a lot closer.

I know you are sick of being lectured by parents and teachers: Don't drink. Don't use drugs. Just say no. But chances are, you—or kids you know—will be caught in situations where they will be tempted to use drugs. Uncle Rob and Tommy learned a hard lesson: Cocaine kills.

Dear God, please help me to be able to say no to drugs. Help me to understand that I don't need drugs to feel good when I have You. Amen.

The First Day

by Holly Seay

"Mom, where is my purple sweater?" yelled Lisa.

"Did you check the laundry room?" called her mother.

The first day of seventh grade, and Lisa wanted everything to be perfect. She had just moved to St. Louis at the beginning of the summer and did not know many people yet. However, she had met a girl named Robin who lived down the street and was also in the seventh grade. Robin and Lisa had become close friends over the summer and were glad they were going to the same school.

Lisa finally got herself together and met Robin at the bus stop. They talked nervously as the bus pulled up in front of school. Lisa hesitated outside the school door, wondering if it would be easier to turn around and go home rather than face the day.

"Come on, Lisa, I'll introduce you to some people I know," prompted Robin.

They walked down the crowded hallway to a boy standing at his locker. "Hi, Kevin, how was your summer?" asked Robin. "I'd like you to meet Lisa. She moved here this summer from Chicago. She lives on my block."

The first bell rang and everyone scurried to their classes, not wanting to be late. "Mind if I walk with you?" Kevin asked Lisa. Kevin introduced Lisa to some of his friends in math class. By the end of class, she was actually beginning to have fun.

You will probably have to face the fear of going to a new school, either moving to a new place, or going from elementary to middle school, or middle school to high school. More than likely your first day won't be as perfect as Lisa's. You may be too scared to try and make new friends right away. It helps to

122

remember that all the other kids are anxious too. Try and be brave enough to talk to other kids. It won't be long before you start enjoying your days.

Lord, please be with me as I attempt to make new friends and go to a new school. Help me to always know that You are my Friend. Amen.

Babysitting—Locked Out!

by Becky Clement

"That darn cat! Why won't he stay in the house," I exclaimed as Petry ventured outside to where the kids and I were playing soccer. I picked him up, put him in the kitchen for the third time, and closed the door tightly. I remembered what Theresa had told me before she left me to watch her two children, Adam and Laura. "When you go outside, make sure the cat doesn't get out or he'll run away." I fixed him this time. There was no way he could get out now, with the door firmly closed.

"Kick the ball, Adam. Oh, nice try!" I cheered, turning back to the little game of soccer we were playing. After 5 more minutes of soccer, Adam and Laura decided to watch a movie.

I turned the knob on the back door and it wouldn't budge. I didn't think it was locked when I closed it, and I didn't have a key. I began to panic. Oh, great, I thought. The first time I babysit for this family and I lock myself out of the house. They'll never let me watch their children again.

I had to think quickly. My house wasn't too far away, but I didn't think I could carry Laura, who was only one-and-a-half, that far and hang on to Adam too. I breathed a quick prayer, asking God to help me. Then we went to a neighbor's house and I asked to use the phone. I called my mom and she came and picked us up. Leaving a note on the front door, I told Theresa what had happened and where we were.

A few hours later Theresa arrived at my house and assured me that the lock was broken and it wasn't my fault. We had a big laugh and she did call me to babysit again.

Dear God, when problems arise in my life, remind me that all I have to do is take them to You in prayer. Amen.

"Open this door or your nine lives are over!"

Peer Pressure

by Scott Radke

"Want some smack?" Chris whispered.

"No," I said. "I don't do that smack."

"Well, how 'bout some weed?" Chris added. "Only fags don't like some kind of upper."

"No! I don't want any!" I yelled. But now it wasn't just Chris. A whole group of guys—all my friends—had gathered round. Chris told them I was being a punk and wouldn't take some free smack. I didn't see how I could get out of it, so I just walked away.

For a while, most of the guys wouldn't talk to me, and the others took every chance to rank on me. It felt like I didn't have any friends. I spent the weekends lying on the couch, watching TV. I started to wonder if it wouldn't be easier to take drugs and be one of the guys, but I knew God kept telling me that I'd done the right thing.

After a few weeks a couple of the guys called and said they didn't like messing around with drugs either. They said they thought Chris was a fool for getting into drugs in the first place.

As the school year went on, more and more of the guys came to hang out with our group instead of Chris. By the time summer rolled around, most of my old friends were back, and Chris and his little drug gang left us alone.

You're probably sick of the words "peer pressure." But this same type of thing could happen to you. Your friends might try and "peer pressure" you into drinking, or trying drugs, or breaking into someone's house, or doing a dozen other things you don't want to do. You are your own person and you can do what you want. Remember, it's likely that if you don't want to do something, most of your group probably doesn't really want to do it either.

If your friends do a lot of things that make you uncomfortable, you may need to make new friends. It will be hard at first, but after God brings them to you, you'll be glad you looked.

Dear God, help me to have a strong faith in You and to make the right decisions. Help me not to be pressured by my friends into doing something that I know, in my heart, is wrong. Amen.